A Cornish Year

David Chapman

To Jenny
With Best Wishes
David

Alison Hodge

First published in 2010 by
Alison Hodge, 2 Clarence Place, Penzance, Cornwall TR18 2QA, UK
www.alison-hodge.co.uk   info@alison-hodge.co.uk

ISBN-13 978-0906720-67-7

British Library Cataloguing-in-Publication Data
A catalogue record for this book is available from the British Library.

Designed and originated by BDP –
Book Development and Production, Penzance, Cornwall.

Printed in China.

Contents

Introduction

A Cornish Year is the follow-up to my first book, *Wild about Cornwall* (2007). In writing this book it has been my aim to produce something which is complementary to it in every way.

Instead of being a guide to places, *A Cornish Year* focuses on activities, organizations, groups, people, types of wildlife, projects and practical work, to name but a few. It is in the style of a diary of my nature activities throughout the year 2008. The tales have been written soon after the event, and the stories are told warts and all. I have written in an informal, yet informative style, which I hope will make it easy to read.

In the main I set out to avoid overlap with *Wild about Cornwall*, so have avoided visiting many of the places featured there. This means that some of the real Cornish wildlife gems, such as Boscregan Farm and Marazion, will not be found within the pages of this book.

Boscregan Farm will not feature in this book. To read about this wonderful place, see Wild about Cornwall.

This book is about getting involved with wildlife, and doing interesting things.

Fortunately, Cornwall is a fantastic county. Its people, its character and its beauty all provide a backdrop against which our natural history thrives, so there was no lack of inspiration to guide me through the year.

To provide as much information as possible, while also allowing the main text of the book to flow, I have inserted a large appendix of further information at the end (see pages 186–92).

So, if you wish to read about the wildlife which is special to Cornwall, or maybe the people who work in conservation in the county; if you want to know what you might do to get more involved with our natural history, or maybe you just want to read about the antics of a mad nature-lover in Cornwall, then read on.

A Twitch in Time

What are you: twitcher, birder, bird-watcher... or just confused?

Of all aspects of our natural history, it is birds that seem to attract the most attention. We need look no further than the one million plus members of the Royal Society for the Protection of Birds (RSPB) for evidence of this. My own interest in the natural history of Britain began with birdwatching, and the experiences I gained of birds and their behaviour have stood me in good stead as a wildlife photographer. My experiences also taught me about the behaviour of the different types of birdwatcher!

Before I discuss the types of birdwatcher, it should be made clear that almost everyone indulging in this hobby keeps lists. Most British birdwatchers keep a British life list – that is a list of birds seen in Britain during their lifetime; they probably also keep a county list, and maybe a garden list.

In the birdwatching world there is no greater maker of lists than a 'twitcher'. The term 'twitcher' is often used to describe all birdwatchers, but it should be used exclusively for one very specialized group. A twitcher is someone who chases rare birds, simply in order to add them to their list, and their aim is to see as many different species of bird as possible in their county, Britain, or even the world. A huge communications network has been established around this growing band of twitchers to help them achieve this. They carry pagers or mobiles, which keep them informed of the latest sightings around the country, and are prepared to drop everything to travel hundreds of miles to add a new bird to their list.

The Hayle Estuary at high tide, seen from The Causeway.

Twitchers almost always occur in groups; they travel together in cars, and then congregate in larger groups at the site of a rare bird. Their dress is variable, but usually a little untidy, from having slept in a car. Trainers are usually the footwear of choice, for speed of access to birdwatching locations, and they always carry a telescope and tripod as well as the obligatory binoculars. Strange beeping noises often emanate from about their person. These, I hope, are due to messages on their pagers. A twitcher will never be seen referring to a bird book in the field; that is very uncool, and probably quite unnecessary when joining a line of birdwatchers all looking at the same thing!

At the other extreme we have the 'birdwatcher'. Birdwatchers are people who have an interest in birds, but who tend to restrict that interest to the times when they go out for a walk in a pleasant part of the countryside, or maybe in their garden. They are probably well-balanced, mentally, and don't necessarily keep lists of everything they see. Birdwatchers mix readily with non-birdwatching people; their dress is often quite colourful, sporting fashionable outdoor clothing rather than camouflage gear, and they can be quite garrulous – often too garrulous to find any decent birds! They will carry binoculars and may have a telescope, which will be in pristine condition; often have a field guide, and aren't afraid to use it in the field.

Spot the difference! The photos on the left are of a Mediterranean gull, those on the right are of a black-headed gull.

Top (L): An adult Mediterranean gull in winter. Note the pale grey-white wing tips, thick-set bill, and black plumage on the head. (Normally in winter there would be slightly less black on the head than this, but more than on the winter-plumaged black-headed gull.) (R): An adult black-headed gull in winter. Note the black feathers in the wing tips, the much slimmer bill, and the black spot behind the eye (which develops into a chocolate brown head in breeding plumage).

Middle (L): An adult Mediterranean gull in flight. Note the plain grey-white wings. (R): An adult winter-plumaged black-headed gull. Note the white leading edge to the wing and the pointed wing tips.

Bottom (L): A juvenile Mediterranean gull, photographed in September. Note the scalloped nature of the plumage on the bird's wing. (R): A juvenile black-headed gull, photographed in September.

The third type of birdwatcher is often known as a 'birder'. Birders are just as dedicated as twitchers, but prefer to find their own birds rather than chasing after reports of rare birds found by others. Birders make copious lists and notes of the birds they see, and report them to the relevant county birdwatching groups for a fuller analysis. They will not be seen with a field guide, but may refer to a guidebook with their notes when at home.

Birders are always well camouflaged, so they may go unnoticed by the casual birdwatcher. They are very quiet, and usually operate alone or in small groups. Rather than travelling the country in search of birds, the birder tends to concentrate on small areas, and may well keep a 'local patch list'. Birders carry telescopes with tripods, and often carry pagers, but use the information gained to help them seek out birds in their local area, and may have them switched off when they are concentrating. An 'off-duty' birder may be confused with a twitcher, since they can occasionally be seen at the site of a rare bird, but only after completing their regular tour of duty.

Listing might seem to be an unnecessary waste of time to the person with a casual interest in birdwatching, but it can add excitement to the hobby. Apart from keeping a life-list of birds, I also try to keep a year list: the fun of a year list is that on 1 January every year it starts again at zero. So every year, on New Year's Day, I plan a long walk which takes me through as many different habitat types as possible. By doing this I can maximize the number of birds I see.

I am lucky that I can walk from my house down to the River Hayle, in Relubbus, and follow the river as far as the Hayle Estuary. Once there, I spend some time on The Causeway, and walk around Carnsew Pool. This walk takes me through farm fields, along the river, through woodland, and around an excellent estuary before walking home and counting up my new list. I normally record between 60 and 70 species on the day, and this simple strategy always serves to reignite my interest in this fascinating hobby.

FOCUS ON THE MEDITERRANEAN GULL

The Mediterranean gull occurs more widely in southern Europe, but is regular in Cornwall in small numbers from late summer through to the end of winter. In Cornwall it most commonly associates with black-headed gulls, so it is sensible to look at the features which separate these two species.

The Mediterranean gull is slightly larger and fuller-bodied with a stouter bill; in all plumages the black-headed gull has a white leading edge to the wing which is lacking in the Mediterranean gull. When at rest, the black-headed gull always shows solid black in the wing tips, a feature lacking from all stages of the Mediterranean gull's plumage except juveniles. Other features depend upon the age of the bird and the season. In winter, an adult Mediterranean gull has a black 'mask', while the black-headed gull has a smudgy dark spot behind its eye.

It is always rewarding to be able to look through a flock of common birds and pick out a rarer one – so what are you waiting for?

Carnsew Pool with the tide rising (above). My first 'tick' of the year was a house sparrow (below), which I had heard in the morning before I got out of bed. One of my personal favourites of the day was a male bullfinch (bottom).

This is exactly what I did today, and this year I saw a grand total of 63 species (see Appendix, page 186) – not a huge number, and many of the regular birds that I might usually expect to see are missing from this tally, but I did make up for that with a couple of excellent records, including both a green-winged teal and a Mediterranean gull on the Hayle Estuary.

Why not plan a walk from your house and see how many birds you can find?

January 3rd

The Cattle Egret

The wonderful thing about birdwatching is that you never quite know what you will see next, and Cornwall is one of the best places in the world for seeing the unexpected. This winter will go down in the annals of birdwatching history for its unprecedented visitation by a large number of cattle egrets.

Being a regular visitor to the 'Cornwall Birds' website, I had noticed that a group of cattle egrets had been roosting at Drift Reservoir and then gathering by day in a field near Halsetown, so that would be where I would go to track them down. On my way there I drove along The Causeway at the Hayle Estuary and was buzzed by a little egret. If I believed in omens then this would be a good one. Fifteen years ago the little egret was rarer in Cornwall than the cattle egret today!

Fortunately I don't believe in omens, so I wasn't surprised when I found that the cattle egrets had decided to spend the day somewhere else. At Halsetown there were just a few cattle and a couple of unhappy-looking birdwatchers. Applying my knowledge of the area and

The little egret (top) is now common in Cornwall. A close-up of one of the cattle egrets in Penwith (above).

my limited understanding of cattle-egret behaviour, I decided to head for Trencrom Hill, where I remembered recently seeing plenty of cattle outdoors. Sure enough, when I got there I found egrets, but they weren't in with the cattle, they were in a field with sheep. Did this leave me with an identification dilemma? Well fortunately not, I know there is no such thing as a 'sheep egret'; obviously they were just cattle egrets with an identity crisis.

A cattle egret with an identity crisis (above, with a winter-plumaged juvenile black-headed gull).

  A cattle egret in breeding plumage (below). Won't it be nice to have these regularly in Cornwall?

The cattle egret is essentially similar to a little egret, but with a few clear differences. First there is the choice of habitat. Little egrets are found on estuaries, creeks, and occasionally rivers and lakes; cattle egrets are found on pasture land with cattle and, obviously, sheep. Unlike the little egret, which spends its time catching small fish from the water, the cattle egret specializes in eating grasshoppers, but will also take worms, larvae and beetles from the animal-fertilized pasture. The plumage of the two species of bird is similar: little egrets are pure white with black bill (in breeding plumage with a blue-grey base), black legs and yellow feet, while cattle egrets are white except for buff plumes on the crown, back and breast in breeding plumage, a yellow bill and greyish legs. One other key difference is in the stature of the two birds. Little egrets are tall and slender compared with the rather small, hunched form of a cattle egret.

The summit of Trencrom has spectacular and far-reaching views. Here we can see Carn Brea rising through an early morning mist.

In the field where I watched the cattle egrets, they were associating with gulls. Their pure white plumage and chicken-like walk made them easily identifiable from their companions. Occasionally, all the birds took off simultaneously, and the broad, arched wings of the cattle egret gave them a graceful, calm air, unlike the frenzied flapping of the gull's wings.

Around the world, cattle egrets are quite common, in fact they could be regarded as one of the world's most cosmopolitan birds, being found in Australia, Asia, Africa, southern Europe and America. They have never bred in Cornwall, or indeed Britain (see Appendix, page 186); the nearest breeding colonies are in southern Spain and France. In the second half of the twentieth century there were only just over 100 records of cattle egrets in the whole of Britain, and that puts some perspective on the 40 or so birds that were in residence in Cornwall during the winter. Their invasion of a new breeding area is not without precedent – in the early part of the twentieth century they were unknown in America, but now they are widespread. This winter may be a precedent for the eventual spread of cattle egrets to our shores. If it is, then I suspect that many people will offer global warming as a cause, but what is more critical is the ability of the cattle egret to thrive in close association with humans – something which it clearly does all over the world.

January 17th

A Tip from the Top

I am not a particularly religious man, though I would like to think that I live by a moral code similar to that of a Christian. My hands occasionally meet in prayer, but I am ashamed to say that it is usually after spending seven or eight hours in a hide waiting for a particular bird to come into view. I understand the lack of morality and double standards implied by what I have just said, but I guess the boredom just gets the better of me, and I imagine I am not alone in offering the occasional plea-prayer.

Anyway, a few weeks ago some prayers that I hadn't even started to make were answered by a pre-emptive strike from the very top. I didn't realize that I wanted to go out and photograph a white-breasted robin until I got a call from a Methodist minister. Imagine my surprise – a telephone call from a man I had never met, telling me of a white-breasted robin on one of his chapel's walls; it's almost enough to make me reconsider my beliefs. Why would he bother about an odd-looking robin? How did he know it was a robin? Why did he contact me?

It transpired that the Revd Andrew Hill, a minister in the Helston Methodist Circuit, is a keen and knowledgeable birdwatcher. We share some very good friends who are Methodists living on the Lizard, where he had spotted the unusual bird, so I felt confident that the white-breasted robin wasn't just the figment of someone's over-active imagination.

My first visit to Ponsongath was not an unparalleled success. I was nearly run over by a tractor driven by a good friend of mine who shall remain nameless; I spent about an hour and a half searching in vain for the robin; a local dog spent the entire time yapping at me through a fence, and about three minutes before I had to leave I spotted the bird and got a photograph only of its bottom disappearing into the undergrowth!

So maybe God wasn't on my side, and he was just teasing me to avenge himself for all of my selfish plea-praying. However, I had seen enough to know that this was a very exciting little bird, its pure white breast and the white flashes in its wings made my encounter every bit as wonderful as spotting a completely new species of bird.

I would have to come back when I could devote more time to the bird, and so it came to pass that on the seventeenth day of January I again headed off to Ponsongath. This time things would be different. I didn't stop to talk to my friend in the tractor; the lady with the dog had gone

A typical robin red-breast in full song (left), and the white-breasted robin singing to an admiring crowd (right).

away on holiday, and after only half an hour I found the robin hopping around in a garden. Of course, walking around a small hamlet with a large lens on a tripod was bound to attract attention, so I did have a bit of a chat with just about every resident of Ponsongath, but it turned out that everyone knew of the white-breasted robin, and one person even suggested that there might be two of them. I was fortunate to meet one local man who had taken to whistling to this particular robin and had noticed that it responded to him, so there I stood with a man whistling into a bush and a white-breasted robin singing back. It was one of my more surreal moments as a wildlife photographer!

Meanwhile, a family who had just stopped to ask what we were doing had walked further along the road and found a second white-breasted robin near the chapel. This was confirmation for the people of Ponsongath that they did indeed have two white-breasted robins.

Now for the science bit... Pure albinism, in which all the bird's feathers are white and its flesh pink, is never common in birds; in most cases of albinism it is just a small area of the bird's feathers that are white – a condition known as partial albinism. True albinism is caused by a recessive gene which has to be present in both parents for it to become visible in an offspring. Partial albinism can be caused by genetics, and in this case the bird will show the same areas of white throughout its lifetime. Other

Partial albinism is most commonly noted in black birds, such as this blackbird (top). Leucism can be seen in this moorhen (above).

causes for a lack of colour pigment in parts of a bird's plumage include sickness or injury affecting their feather follicles, or even diet affecting their ability to generate colour pigment, but these cases more commonly produce pale birds – a condition known as leucism – or birds with patchy white feathers which might change after a moult. It seems that the two partial albino robins were first seen in the summer of 2007, and so it is likely they are siblings from the same parents. Given the extensive nature of their white plumage, I suspect that the cause of their albinism is genetic.

January 26th

The Big Garden Birdwatch

For budding birders, nutty naturalists and conversant conservationists everywhere, the last weekend in January can mean only one thing: The Big Garden Birdwatch. This is the biggest bird survey of the year, organized every year since 1979 by the RSPB. From a small beginning, a mighty survey has grown, which now regularly attracts over 400,000 entries. Considering that this is often a family affair with two or three people watching birds for each survey form entered, I reckon that must amount to around a million people watching birds with the same goal on one weekend.

The rules are simple. Each participant must choose a one-hour period to spend watching birds in their garden on the last weekend of January. For each species seen, the maximum number of birds of that species seen at the same time during that hour is recorded. So if four house sparrows come down to feed at the beginning and then eight come to feed at the same time later on, the number recorded for house sparrows is 'eight'. This system is intended to prevent us counting the same bird more than once, and to provide a standardized approach.

I thought the most appropriate way to spend this year's Big Garden Birdwatch was with a member of the RSPB staff, so I invited myself round to the home of Jenny Parker, Assistant Warden for the Cornwall Reserves, in St Just.

Jenny has a small, attractive terraced house, typical of many people in the county, though what is not typical about this place is the view. From her bedroom window she can see over farm fields to the sea, with Longships Lighthouse and even the Isles of Scilly visible on a good day. This would make an interesting place to do a Garden Birdwatch; maybe we could set up a telescope and count guillemot on the list? Alas, no, the birds have to be within the garden, so we weren't even allowed to count the herring gulls that flew low over the house, let alone the guillemots flying out to sea.

I asked Jenny what her most exciting garden bird record was. In the eight months she has lived there, the best record was of a goldfinch.

*Jenny Parker tops up the feeders (above).
The goldfinch (below) is Jenny's best
ever record in her garden, and who
could argue with that?*

I began to feel a bit guilty, because we regularly have flocks of around 20 goldfinches in our garden, but The Big Garden Birdwatch is not about concentrating on big gardens. Maybe it should really be called the Garden Big Birdwatch, but then I suppose people would only do it if they had big birds in their gardens! All surveys are of equal importance, so if you spend an hour and see only one bird in a windblown garden in West Penwith, that information is just as important as someone who sees 25 varieties in a wooded garden in Saltash.

As well as providing a vital source of fresh water for her birds, Jenny has feeders containing mixed seed and peanuts, and she puts some seed on the ground. She tries to keep her bird food as far from danger as possible. There are lots of cats in the area, so to prevent her birds being hunted, she cuts back her shrubs at their base so that they do not form a hiding place for the felines, and she puts out seed in the middle of the lawn so that birds can see if cats are around. As well as the bird food in Jenny's garden, she told me that her neighbour had fat balls suspended in the tree overhanging the perimeter wall, and we could borrow them for the purposes of the survey. Even I couldn't come up with a quick enough response to that line!

I was a little taken aback when Jenny invited me up to her bedroom: the look on my face must have been enough to convince her that further explanation might be a good idea. 'The view is much better from the bedroom window,' and sure enough it was. From there we could see clearly into the evergreen

The chaffinch (top) is now top bird in Cornwall's gardens.
The great tit (above) is present in the vast majority of our gardens.

For me, the starling was the most fascinating bird of the hour.

hedgerow at the bottom of the garden as well as around the small lawn and feeders, while also having a much better view of any passing guillemots!

The hour passed remarkably quickly, despite there not being a huge variety of birds. The two most numerous species, which tie in with the national and county results for every year that the survey has taken place, were starling and house sparrow. The starlings looked resplendent in their glossy purple and green plumage. For me, listening to their constant chattering was one of the highlights. Jenny recalled that her first encounter with bird-feeding in a garden was when she was about eleven or twelve years old. The bird that still lived in her memory was the house sparrow. The male, with his chestnut back, grey head and black bib; the female, with her delightful, pale supercilium, and together, their antics, playfulness, aggression and cheerful, chirpy calls. Taking part in this sort of survey does bring home just how interesting and invigorating watching 'common' birds can be.

Sadly, neither house sparrows nor starlings are as common in gardens as they were in 1979. The house sparrow has declined by more than 50 per cent and the starling by more than 75 per cent in that time. The other biggest loser is the song thrush, but some species – notably wood pigeon, collared dove and the tit family – have increased in numbers.

Our tally for the hour ended with just nine species on the list, and only five of those finished with more than one bird recorded. In fact, it wasn't until we had completed the form that things really started to happen, with a robin and a pair of blackbirds hopping around on the lawn, but we couldn't count them!

February 2nd

Raindrops on Snowdrops

The 2nd of February is Candlemas Day – an ancient festival marking the mid-point of winter. It was previously known as the 'Feast of Lights' and the 'Festival Day (or mass) of the Candles', and celebrated the lengthening days associated with this time of year. Candles are of great significance, being used by Christians to remind them of the light that Jesus brought to the world. On this day, all the candles that were to be used in church for the coming year were brought into

You organize an outdoor event, and what happens?

the church and blessed. Candlemas is also the date of the Feast of the Purification of the Virgin Mary, and was once seen as the end of the Christmas season, when Christmas decorations should be taken down.

Many superstitions have grown up around Candlemas Day, and, since this is mid-winter, it should come as no surprise that some are linked to predicting the weather for the remainder of this season:

If Candlemas Day be fair and bright,
Winter will have another fight.
If Candlemas Day brings cloud and rain,
Winter won't come again.

Today was wet and extremely windy, so the theory is that winter should now be at an end, though in truth we have seen little of winter weather at all.

The snowdrop is often associated with Candlemas as its flowers can usually be found on this day. Their blooms act as a religious symbol of

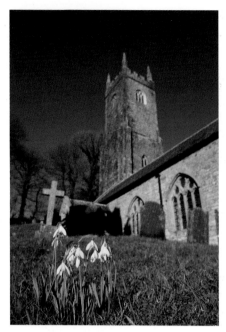

Snowdrops tend to be most common at ecclesiastical sites, such as here at Altarnun (left). They look delicate, but are well equipped to deal with frosty conditions (right).

Candlemas, and were once used to decorate chapels and churches on this day. This association is still obvious today, as snowdrops are more likely to be found growing in churchyards and around old religious sites than anywhere in the wider countryside. Given that they flower in the coldest part of the year, the snowdrop has been adopted in gardens and stately homes around the county, and one annual celebration of this wonderful flower takes place at Pencarrow House, near Bodmin, on the Sunday nearest to Candlemas Day.

Each year, a snowdrop walk is organized at Pencarrow, and today I braved the wet weather to take part. The house and gardens of Pencarrow are beautiful. I have visited at many different times of year, and I must confess that my favourite is early May, when bluebells and ramsons bedeck the grassland near the house. Snowdrops are found at only two or three locations around the gardens, but it was pleasant to be able to stroll around and have a cup of tea in the café.

This year the weather was relatively mild, but even in Cornwall the snowdrop has to be able to resist the effects of frosts. Lying dormant underground as a bulb, the snowdrop has the ability to emerge quickly at a time of year when most flowers have no choice but to wait. The chisel-like leaves are able to penetrate frosty ground, and a leaf-like structure above the flowers protects them as they force their way through. But

Snowdrops penetrate the sodden ground, while people with raincoats make the most of it at Pencarrow. The grounds of Pencarrow are wonderful for bluebells and ramsons in early May (below).

even with the ability to grow quickly, snowdrops still need to be able to withstand the formation of ice inside their stems. Most plants would wilt and die in such conditions, but snowdrops are able to withdraw water from their cells and store it in voids, so that when it freezes it doesn't cause damage to their fragile cell structure. Their nodding heads, which close at night, open in the morning to reveal a supply of nectar, but attracting insects at this time of year is difficult. Snowdrops certainly have the ability to produce seed, but their reproduction is more often through the production of further bulbs, and so their distribution changes very slowly. This is another reason why snowdrops are still found close to where they were centuries ago.

February 5th

Just Cruising

An avocet's up-turned bill.

To many people, the most appealing of all of Cornwall's wading birds is the avocet. The scientific name of this delightful bird just about sums it up in two words: *Recurvirostra avosetta*, which literally means 'a graceful bird with up-turned beak'. The 'graceful bird', or *avosetta*, has been abbreviated to form the common name by which we now know this species.

The avocet was once a common breeding bird in Britain, but it ceased breeding in the middle of the nineteenth century, the last pair being recorded in Kent. Later on, when the marshes of East Anglia were flooded as a form of defence during the Second World War, the avocet was attracted back again. The RSPB selected this species as its emblem because of the avocet's success in breeding at Minsmere, one of their reserves in Suffolk.

Due to increased awareness and more wildlife-friendly management of wetland reserves on the east coast, the avocet has now increased its range significantly, but it does not occur in Cornwall as a breeding bird. Our only chance of seeing one is during winter, because the birds that breed in eastern England migrate south and west to stay on the Exe and Tamar estuaries from November to February. Significant numbers of these birds have been occurring on the Tamar Estuary since the 1960s, and we can now see up to about 400 birds during very cold weather.

The avocet is black and white, and is a relatively large wader but, unlike the oystercatcher, it is slim and long legged. Its ridiculously upturned bill could look incongruous but, maybe because it is so slender, it somehow befits the rest of the bird. The avocet's feeding movements have evolved to suit the shape of its bill (or vice versa): it sweeps its head from side to side in long, flowing movements, a bit like a ballet dancer turning from side to side with flowing gestures of the arms. In this way, the avocet col-

A boatful of birdwatchers on the Tamar cruise (above), and a view from the cruise boat – the only view of Devon you will see in this book (below)!

lects creatures from the water's surface, the shape of its beak enabling it to keep its head above water while having a good proportion of its beak just below the surface. But in fact, the avocet can turn its head to many different kinds of feeding, including probing into the mud for worms.

In winter, avocets often gather in loose flocks; they need space in order to feed, but they enjoy the close proximity of others of their kind. Their frequently uttered, high-pitched *pleet-pleet* calls vary in volume according to their level of excitement and their proximity to others. When disturbed they take flight in unison, their long blue legs trailing even further behind them than their bills protrude in front. There is a fine line between graceful and gangly, and the avocet, in flight, must come fairly close to it, but overall this is a delightful bird to watch, because it is so very different from the other waders with which it coexists.

Interest in the avocet in Cornwall has been increased recently by the re-establishment of birdwatching cruises around the Tamar Estuary. Five

*Plenty of other waders were seen on the estuary, including curlews (left).
Even graceful birds can get into strange positions sometimes (right)! The great
northern diver (below) was a surprise find under the Tamar Bridges.*

Trematon Castle seen from the Lynher River.

or six cruises take place most winters, offering a most unusual and very comfortable way to watch birds in an otherwise difficult environment.

Today I went out on one of these cruises. The weather was cold and grey for the most part, but the hospitality and camaraderie were warm and colourful. The leader of the trip was wired up for sound so that everyone on the boat could be kept informed as to what was seen. This commentary was of great value to novices in birdwatching, and was also informative enough to be interesting to those with a greater knowledge.

I suspect that today was fairly typical: the open-air deck of the boat crammed with people as we cruised up-river, when the air of excitement and anticipation were evident in the crowd scanning the muddy shores of the Tamar. As we turned to head back down the river, the emphasis changed to a warm cup of tea and biscuits from the on-board canteen. Once we were back under the famous Tamar Bridges, we then headed up the Lynher River, where everyone made their way up on to the top deck, to be rewarded by a good view of four spoonbills, which, like the cattle egrets, might one day breed in Cornwall. All in all we saw 141 avocets, or so I am told, though I suspect that the experience of the trip will last in my mind longer than the views of the avocets.

February 6th

A Seal's Approval

The rendezvous was planned for 7.30 a.m. at Gwithian Beach, near the mouth of the Red River. I had arrived a little early and had time to take in the atmosphere of the place at this wonderful time of day. I was unsure what to expect but, for once, the weather was excellent. The sun hadn't yet risen above the dunes behind me, but as I looked out to sea over Godrevy Lighthouse, the pink hues in the sky hinted at its imminent appearance. The waves that crashed on to the beach were a remnant of the storm that had passed over a few days ago, but the breeze was still brisk, and the breakers impressive.

This morning, four grey seals from the National Seal Sanctuary were to be released here, and I wondered how they would cope in this hostile environment. After being found stranded around various parts of the county's coastline during the autumn, these seals had known nothing but the cosy pools of the Sanctuary and a daily ration of easy fish.

Slowly, people started to arrive. There were the people who had found the seals; those who had transported them; some of the helpers who had looked after them at the Seal Sanctuary; a few interested others like me, and, finally, the people who were transporting them here for release. The seals were carried here in a trailer, towed by a four-wheel drive vehicle which pulled them all the way down on to the soft sand of the beach. In the trailer, the seals were calm, no doubt wondering what fate might befall them here this morning. Any fear they might have had seemed to be overcome by curiosity; their senses of smell and hearing were surely enough to let them know that they were about to return to their natural environment. I made eye contact with them through the wire sides of the trailer, and as the strong smell of their breath drifted out to greet me, I realized that I had never before been this close to a seal.

The engine of the four-wheel drive was extinguished as the back of the trailer was lowered. All four seals hesitated momentarily before beginning the steep descent of the trailer's ramp. Once on wet sand, three of them saw the surf and made a quick decision about which way to go, heading off speedily in the right direction. The fourth was far more reluctant; once on the sand he repeatedly turned to look at the friends who had nursed him for the last few months. The others had disappeared when eventually Kitto made it to the surf, and even then he was to make several appear-

The grey seals arrive on Gwithian Beach from the National Seal Sanctuary (above). This is as close as I have ever been to a grey seal (below).

ances along the beach before leaving for good. Evidently it is always the males that are more reluctant to make a break for it, obviously preferring to be mollycoddled!

The whole experience was profoundly moving. I found the fact that so many people were involved quite inspiring, and this was just the first release of the 'season'. A typical year might see between 40 and 50 seals brought to the Seal Sanctuary. The seals are kept only as long as they need to be before being released, so that they have as little human contact as possible.

Before being released, the seals have to reach a threshold weight of 40 kilograms. Our four today were between 50 and 55 kilograms, which gave us reassurance that they would have time to settle into their new environment before needing to find food.

A crowd of admirers watches as the grey seals are released (above).
Kitto was the only reluctant seal, but even he eventually made it (below).

Grey seal pups are born on the beaches and in coves in autumn.

All seals that are released are marked in some way so that they can be identified in the future. These four seals had small tags on their back flippers. By looking out for them in the future, we can learn a little about how successful these creatures are. One encouraging piece of news was reported last year when a seal named Puffa, which had been released in 2000, gave birth to a pup. This is the first time that we know of a released seal raising her own pup, but that isn't to say that it hasn't happened without us knowing!

One of the most reliable places to watch seals in Cornwall is at Mutton Cove, just to the east of Godrevy Point, where it is quite common to see them hauled out on the inaccessible beach at low tide. They give birth to their pups from late August to early December, and last year about thirteen were born here. I know that when I go to the cliffs above Mutton Cove in future I will be paying particularly close attention to the numbers on the flipper tags, to see if I can spot one of 'my' seals.

February 14th

Love is in the Air

My homage to Lorna Tremayne, and probably not as good a photo as hers, despite my camera costing rather more!

Since it is Valentine's Day today, I decided to be romantic and take my wife, Sarah, to one of Cornwall's finest gardens. She might have thought that we were going to enjoy walking through the gardens and looking at flowers, but I had an ulterior, amphibious motive.

Last year I was captivated by a photograph taken by Lorna Tremayne, the marketing and publicity manager at The Lost Gardens of Heligan. The gardens are obviously not as busy in the winter as they are in the spring and summer, so they designed a leaflet whose cover showed a frog on a path by the pond in the Italian Garden. I have to admire anyone who thinks they can attract people to a garden by printing a leaflet with a frog on the cover, but it obviously worked because we wouldn't have been there today if it weren't for that photo.

The Lost Gardens of Heligan provide a wonderful diversity of habitats for wildlife, and for that reason I featured this location in my book *Wild About Cornwall*, so I won't go into detail about the gardens and the work done to protect wildlife; suffice to say, you won't be disappointed if you visit. This is about our amphibious friends.

In Cornwall, it isn't uncommon to find frogspawn as early as December, but generally it is early in February that most frogs leave their hibernation sites under logs or in holes where they have spent the entire winter without eating. After waking, they hop or crawl up to half a mile until

*A pair of common toads get romantic in the Italian Garden (above).
A frog sits among spawn (below).*

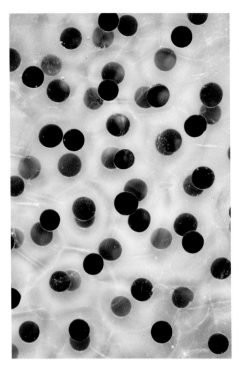

Fresh frogspawn.

they reach what is usually their own birth pond in search of a mate. The males, which are slightly darker than the females, tend to arrive a little earlier than the females, and they sit in wait for them, gently croaking as they do so.

A couple of weeks later it is the turn of the common toad. Larger in size, and with a warty skin, the toad is more likely to walk than hop, and this is one of the easiest ways to identify them. Males are smaller than females, but there is some variability, and even other toads can make mistakes when selecting a partner! Fortunately, the males utter a 'release call' – a small croak to warn off other males – the deeper the croak, the more dominant the toad.

Females of both species tend to attract great interest from a large number of males. The first male attaches himself to her back in a hug known as amplexus – literally a 'fond hug'. Their specially adapted thumbs help them to keep a grip under the armpits of their slippery partners. Where females are outnumbered by males, several males might try to hold on to one female, and a sparring mass of croaking toads or frogs will ensue.

When spawning takes place, toads lay their eggs, two wide, in a long string wrapped around vegetation in the pond. These strings can contain as many as 3,000–4,000 eggs. Frogs lay theirs in a single clump of up to 2,000 eggs, the jelly substrate surrounding the eggs expanding, through absorption of water, after it is laid. Think of the relief that the female must feel when spawning is complete and she can head off to feed. The males, however, tend to stay around to see if they can sow their seed further!

At Heligan today we found both frogs and toads in the Italian Garden, but it seemed that most of the frogs had finished spawning, and it was the turn of the toads to be in amplexus. I'm ashamed to say that Lorna, with her inexpensive compact, managed to capture the spirit of the frog better than I did with my expensive camera equipment. I show you my photos from the day here. To see hers, you will have to visit Heligan.

Coincidentally, when I returned home, I was contacted by a friend who had found frogspawn in not much more than a puddle of water where it would not survive. I decided to collect it and raise it in a fish tank in my porch. The next few weeks provided me with the opportunity to photo-

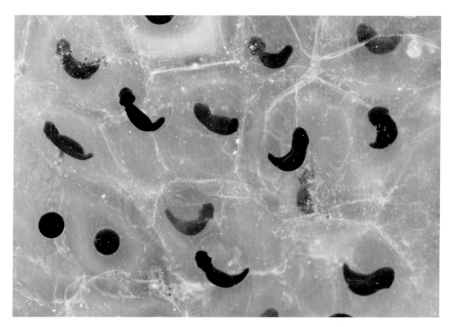

My frogspawn begins to develop (above), and the tadpoles grow legs (below).

graph frogspawn and tadpoles before releasing the tiny frogs in my garden pond in early April. I hope that my new pond will play host to masses of frogs in future years.

The frogs emerge from the water just before release (above). A pond and wildlife habitat form part of the wildlife project at Heligan (right).

From Croaks to Crocuses

Crocuses and daffodils flower together.

On reflection, taking my wife to look at mating frogs on Valentine's Day might not have been the most romantic gesture possible, but let's hope that a trip to a graveyard in St Teath will make up for it!

The middle of February is crocus season, and though crocuses are not technically wildflowers, the ones around the church in St Teath have been around long enough to merit their honorary inclusion in my unofficial 'Wildflowers of Cornwall' list. Anyway, I don't care about their status, what attracted me to St Teath was the spectacle created in this attractive churchyard by literally thousands of crocuses.

I have been to see the crocuses at St Teath before, but never really had the timing quite right. Today, I think I saw them at their zenith, and a memorable sight it was too.

This churchyard is not alone in being a valuable one for wildlife; in fact there is a national project, The Living Churchyards, which has many groups operating at county level, including one in Cornwall. Its aims are to enhance the wildlife habitat of churchyards through conservation management, while creating an atmosphere of benefit to grieving visitors, to aid the understanding of our natural and cultural heritage, and to enhance the amenity value of churchyards.

The church at St Teath.

In some cities, churchyards and parks are the only green areas, and it is no wonder that local people have been keen to protect them. In Cornwall, where we have so many wonderful wildlife sites, it may seem unnecessary to protect the natural history in churchyards, but exploring a little further has made me realize how very important these places are. When put into their historical context, it shouldn't be at all surprising that churchyards have become invaluable to wildlife.

Most of our ecclesiastical buildings have been around for centuries, and much of their surrounding land has been intact for millennia, with churches being built and rebuilt in the same location for generation after generation. Some of our wildlife can be incredibly slow to take advantage of new settings, but once established may thrive if the conditions are beneficial. The snowdrop is a good example, but so too are the many species of lichen that we can always find growing around churches. Lichens are slow growers, but they can take advantage of the undisturbed walls of churches, their boundary hedges, and the gravestones themselves. To illustrate the significance of churchyards for lichens, the British Lichen Society has undertaken surveys which reveal that of the 1,700 British species of lichen, over 300 can be found growing in churchyards.

The trees that grow around churches are often the oldest in a particular area. One tree in particular, the yew, has a close association with burial grounds, which dates back to pre-Christian times; indeed, since some yew trees certainly live longer than 2,000 years, there are even individual trees which pre-date Christian times.

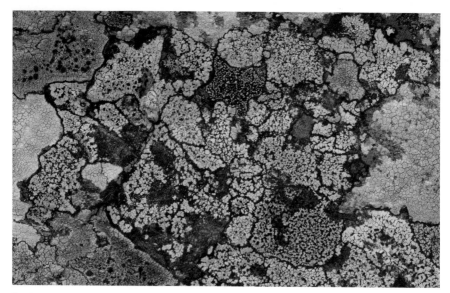

Lichens, such as these map lichens, grow on gravestones (above).
Minster church, near Boscastle, is one of many churches to take part in the Living Churchyards Project (below).

Another classic association between churches and wildlife can be seen, or heard, in the belfries. I refer, of course, to bats. Traditionally, bats would have found roost sites in tree cavities and caves, but with the demise of much of our woodland, some species of bat took to the roof spaces of houses and other buildings. Bats have fared badly in Britain over recent years, partly because modern houses do not tend to allow them to gain access. Old buildings such as churches, with their tall spires and often accessible roof spaces, can offer them a valuable sanctuary. Combine this with insect-rich churchyards and we can see that churches offer one of the most important opportunities to safeguard the future of this fantastic group of creatures.

Birds also find churchyards to their liking. In a survey undertaken

Churches and churchyards are great for wildflowers and wildlife. Cowslips at St Uny church, Lelant (above); a spotted flycatcher at St Enoder (below).

by the British Trust for Ornithology, an impressive 39 species of bird were recorded breeding in twelve churchyards. All of the typical garden birds can be found, but one or two could be said to be churchyard specialists. The spotted flycatcher enjoys clearings between trees in which to hunt; it nests in old walls, and likes to perch out in the open to look for insects. Where better than the churchyard? I have certainly seen them around several Cornish churches.

The Living Churchyard project and, specifically, Cornwall's Living Churchyards, are supported by a wide range of people and groups. In Cornwall, the project is headed by the Cornwall Wildlife Trust (CWT). Churches across the county have taken on board the spirit of the project, but no other can quite match the crocus spectacle of St Teath.

Scandal of the Killing Nets

The dead common dolphin on the beach at Gunwalloe Fishing Cove.

Today, a day off work to enjoy a bit of good Cornish food and a walk along a wonderful piece of coastline near Gunwalloe Fishing Cove turned out to be what I hope will be one of the saddest days of the year. There had been a strong south-westerly wind blowing for about a week, so I wondered if anything unusual might have been stranded here. I was thinking that there might be some goose barnacles, and I had joked with Sarah that there might even be some cocaine, since there had already been several packages washed up on Cornish beaches in the previous few weeks.

We did find something of interest, but not what I would have wanted. Right at the end of the beach, just before the rocks of Halzephron headland, at approximately the mid-tide level, was a common dolphin: a once vibrant and beautiful creature had died at sea and been washed ashore. This unfortunate creature had been spotted by a pair of ravens which honked in annoyance as I approached.

Unfortunately, occurrences of dead dolphins on the coastline of the South West have increased in recent years. In 1995, there were just 24 found on the shoreline, while in the first few years of the twenty-first

Caroline Curtis records details and voice on her video camera (above).
The dolphin's beak reveals monofilament net stuck in the wound (below).

century, as many as 255 in 2003 have been washed ashore in a single year. Unbeknown to me, there had been a peak in the number of creatures found in the previous few days, with nine common dolphins and a porpoise occurring in the last week or so.

'My' common dolphin was going to be the latest statistic in a long line of fatalities. Fortunately, I had my mobile phone with me today, and in it I have the number of the CWT strandings volunteer line. This 24-hour telephone line has been established by volunteers who, in the long term, are working to prevent this number of dolphin deaths by collecting evidence of the cause of death from the corpses. Not a pretty job, and the volunteers spend a huge amount of time and money travelling around the county in pursuit of their goal.

Within two hours, volunteer Caroline Curtis had arrived on the scene, and on this occasion I had waited for her to see exactly what the volunteers do. She started with a video camera, filming every part of the dolphin

A view along the beach towards Porthleven from Gunwalloe Fishing Cove.

and discussing any marks that might provide evidence of how it had died. She progressed to taking still photos of key signs of damage, and also took measurements of various parts of the dolphin.

Caroline told me that this dolphin was a male, and that it was a big animal so it had lived to a good age, unlike many that had been washed ashore recently, all of which had been females. We discussed the likely cause of death, and I was reassured by the measured and reserved way in which she weighed up the possibilities. Even though there were strands of monofilament net stuck in the wounds on the animal's beak, she did not want to commit to the exact cause of death.

There are two main causes of such deaths around the Cornish coast, but before I discuss these I will highlight some differences in the behaviour of the cetaceans involved. The three species which are generally at risk and are of primary concern are: common dolphin; harbour porpoise, and bottlenose dolphin. Of these, the porpoise and bottlenose dolphins are most likely to be encountered close to shore; the common dolphin is more likely to be found further out to sea.

One of the causes of cetacean deaths – the one least mentioned in nationwide publicity because of its sensitivity to our own fishermen – is the monofilament gill-net fishery carried out close to shore. This is a regulated industry, but it is only controlled to prevent catching salmonids (salmon and trout), and the fishermen are largely following government regulations. Despite this adherence to the law, the gill nets are trapping large numbers of harbour porpoises. Evidence of this comes directly from distressed fishermen, and from the strandings of dead porpoises with the telltale signs of gill-net damage. It doesn't take a great mind to work out what is happening: the gill nets trap fish; the fish attract porpoises; the porpoises become entangled and drown. In fact, they suffocate rather than drown, since their central nervous system prevents them from choosing to breathe when under water.

This is a sensitive issue, but almost everyone involved is working towards possible solutions. The use of 'pingers', which can be attached to gill nets and emit a sound that deters cetaceans, has been trialled, and under new European Union (EU) regulations these must now be fitted to all gill nets used by larger fishing vessels (over 12 metres).

The other, and major, cause of deaths is easier to discuss because 'we' are not largely to blame. By 'we', I mean 'we British', though I don't suppose the idea of nationality means much to the dolphins. I refer to 'Bass pelagic pair-trawling' – the system of pulling a huge, mid-water net (about 140 metres wide, 60 metres deep, and 280 metres long) for an average of seven and a half hours between two trawlers through the biggest shoals of fish that can be found.

This is usually undertaken outside the twelve-mile coastal zone which is controlled by our own government, so it is a European issue. The teams of trawlers are also European, with most coming from France, and some from Spain, Holland and Denmark; the UK element of the fleet comprises a small number of boats from Scotland only.

The bass fishery is a non-quota fishery, with minimal regulations, and fishermen are targeting the spawning grounds of this species where huge shoals aggregate to breed. No doubt you've heard the word 'unsustainable' used frequently, but don't get bored with it: through this ridiculous strategy, bass numbers are now being seriously depleted.

The common dolphins feed on similar prey species to the bass (herring, sprat, pilchard, etc.), and naturally use the same areas in which to feed. Unfortunately, the nets used to plunder our seas for bass are indiscriminate. We have long known, through records of strandings, that hundreds of common dolphins are killed by this fishery each year. Evidence comes in the form of badly damaged dolphin bodies washed up on our shore. Their beaks are usually broken by their own actions as they struggle to break free of the nets, while slowly but inevitably suffocating; their bodies often sliced into parts by fishermen either trying to free their nets, or attempting to cover up the sinister side to their work.

Those dolphins washed up on our shore are just the tip of the iceberg; not all of the dolphins killed become stranded; the statistics that I have quoted thus far are not indicative of the true devastation of our actions. In attempting to trial an escape hatch for dolphins to be placed in trawlers' nets – which, incidentally, has failed miserably, observations were made on a pair of trawlers fishing for bass. The result was devastating. One hundred and sixty-nine dolphins were caught by one pair of trawl-

I had hoped to find some goose barnacles after the stormy weather.

ers during the short trial. Multiply this by the length of the bass-fishing season, and then again by the number of boats at work, and you will see that not only are the bass stocks in danger of collapse, but so too is the long-term population of 'common' dolphins.

Greenpeace now estimates that of the total population of 75,000 common dolphins in the Celtic Sea, approximately 4,000 are dying in the nets of bass pair trawlers each year. The government is also concerned about the deaths; its figures suggest that, on average, one dolphin is caught with every two hauls of the nets in this particular fishery.

Our government has now taken unilateral action, and has banned pair-trawling from the twelve-mile zone around our coast. This is a bold step, which will send out a clear message of intent to the rest of Europe, but unfortunately won't save many dolphins. It is clear that people in areas where dolphins and porpoises are regularly washed ashore have a strong desire for change. Having spent time with Caroline Curtis, and having witnessed first-hand the damage caused to dolphins during the terrifying and drawn-out period of distress and torment leading to their death, all I can say is that I feel ashamed.

Most of the dolphins and porpoises washed ashore in this recent spate had been killed in monofilament gill nets. The evidence for this came from observations made by volunteers, and also through at least one post-mortem, for when the beach inspection is complete the animals are either buried or taken for further inspection. In the case of 'my' dolphin, we were beaten by the tide, and could do nothing except tag the animal to make sure it wasn't reported again should it be washed ashore anywhere else.

There are specific things that we can do to help protect the dolphins (see Appendix, page 187). We can't just bury our heads in the sand and pretend it isn't happening. These are intelligent and wonderful creatures, which have as much right to their space on this earth as we have to ours. We must learn to respect that right.

March 19th

From the Caribbean with Love

Just as January was dominated by birdwatching events, it seems that March is becoming 'Marine Month'. Today I visited the Blue Reef Aquarium in Newquay, but not simply for a look around their aquariums.

On 1st February, a dog walker in Bude found a rare turtle washed up on a beach. Fortunately, despite this turtle being apparently dead, the person had the presence of mind to alert the RSPCA, who then contacted the British Divers Marine Life Rescue (BDMLR). Volunteer Dave Jarvis was prepared to drive about 50 miles to North Cornwall to pick up the animal, and once on site found that there were still signs of life.

He applied basic turtle first aid, which included tipping the animal up slightly so that any fluids trapped in the creature's lungs could drain through its mouth, and wrapping the turtle in a wet towel to keep it moist and at the same temperature at which it was found. He then drove it to the Blue Reef Aquarium in Newquay.

Introducing Dink, who along with James survived to be released in Gran Canaria. (Top: in his heated swimming pool.)

My name is James.

Once at the Blue Reef, the turtle received very special care. It was placed in a tank of shallow water at roughly the same temperature as the sea in which it had been found. Although turtles, being cold-blooded reptiles, need a warmer sea in order to survive, if their surrounding water temperature changes suddenly, they may be killed. Over the next week or so, the turtle's water temperature was increased by 2°C per day, from 10°C to 25°C. Meanwhile, the turtle was tube-fed with rehydrating fluids and puréed squid; it was given antibiotics because vets thought it had pneumonia as well as hypothermia; it was scrubbed with antiseptic each day to treat lesions on its shell, and was X-rayed to check it internally for blockages to its digestive and respiratory systems.

This final point is the cause of many turtle deaths, and it is often us humans who are responsible. I wouldn't mind betting that most of us have taken part in a charity balloon race, or have watched with glee as thousands of small balloons are released to mark the opening of an event. These balloons have to end up somewhere, and many of them, along with millions of plastic bags, end up in the sea. Turtles eat a variety of foods, but their favourite is the jellyfish and, unfortunately, they are not always able to distinguish between a rubbery-looking, sac-like jellyfish and a rubbery-looking, sac-like balloon or plastic bag. Plastic and rubber are indigestible and lead the turtle to die through suffocation or starvation. Fortunately, 'our' turtle was clear of any such problems.

This turtle was given a number by DEFRA, and because it was '007' staff decided to name it James Bond; the fact that it was a female didn't

Among the other creatures at the Blue Reef Aquarium, is this cuttlefish.

stop them! James was, in fact, a loggerhead turtle – an exceptionally rare find in Cornwall, because this particular type of turtle has no control over its body temperature, and would be sure to die if it couldn't find warmer waters. Over the course of a year, there may be about six loggerheads recorded in Cornwall, as opposed to about 30 leatherback turtles, a species which can control its own temperature to some degree.

Those numbers are for typical years, but in the first ten weeks of this year there have been nineteen loggerheads washed up on the shores of Cornwall – a fact which can probably be attributed to the intense storms that we have experienced over this period. These turtles have been carried up from the Caribbean or other areas of warmer waters in the Atlantic. They would have become increasingly lethargic, and at the mercy of the elements as their internal temperatures dropped. In fact, I learned that two further turtles had been brought to the Blue Reef Aquarium, and one, a small loggerhead named Dink, perhaps only one or two years old, has survived, and is doing well.

From her size – about 50 cm long – it is thought that James is between 10 and 15 years old. James has increased her weight from 15 kg to about 18 kg in the first six weeks of intensive care at The Blue Reef, and staff are already thinking of the next phases in her rehabilitation. One vital step in her treatment is to provide her with more varied feeding strategies to prepare her for the real world. The final phase will involve a flight to the Canaries, at the expense of the Blue Reef Aquarium. Once in the Canaries, the turtles are kept for a few days in a special aquarium, for a final programme of health checks, before being released into the wild – a process which has been undertaken successfully three times previously.

It seems that James the loggerhead might be one turtle that will 'never say die', but let's hope that the bond between him and the staff at the Blue Reef Aquarium can be successfully broken, and once James is released he won't need a 'Dr No' more!

The Great Easter Egg Hunt

The egg-case of a blonde ray (top), and the classic mermaid's purse with tendrils – the egg-case of a nursehound or lesser-spotted catshark (above).

Everybody goes egg-hunting at Easter, though I must confess that when I agreed to take part in today's activity I thought there might have been some chocolate involved!

I should have realized when Rory Goodall, the walk leader, told me there should be plenty of eggs around 'because of all the stormy weather we have been having'. This is certainly true, we seem to have had strong winds for the last six weeks or so, including some of the most severe storms I can remember. This is probably the reason why so many of my recent engagements have been marine based.

Rory Goodall is best known in the county for his voluntary work with the CWT, and for the fact that he has established a wildlife tour business, Elemental Tours, which takes people around the West Cornwall area by land and sea. On this occasion he was taking a walk on behalf of the Shark Trust, and if I had known that before agreeing to take part, I might have realized that we were actually going to be looking for eggs made by sharks, skates and rays rather than Cadbury.

Rory Goodall (above right) shows a group how to identify an egg-case.

The Shark Trust is a charity, and was established in 1997. It works to promote the conservation of sharks, skates and rays, which are known collectively as 'elasmobranchs'. The word 'elasmobranch' relates to the plate-like gills in this group of fish, *elasmos* being Greek for 'beaten metal', and *bragkhia* for gills.

It may surprise you to know that over 21 species of shark and fifteen types of skate and ray have been recorded around Britain, and Cornwall is a great place for them. Most sharks are viviparous, which means they give birth to live young (*vivus* being Latin for 'alive' and *parere* meaning to 'bring forth'), but a few, including the nursehound (aka bull huss) and lesser-spotted catshark, lay eggs. These two species are often referred to as dogfish but are, in fact, both catsharks, since dogfish give birth to live young. All skates and rays are oviparous, which means they produce eggs. The eggs of elasmobranchs are known familiarly as 'mermaid's purses', because of their pocket-like shape and straps at either end.

These eggs are laid either in the sand or attached to seaweed on the seabed. Inside the egg-case, a single egg develops into a fully developed miniature version of the adult fish, which may take up to nine months to hatch. Eventually, the egg-cases break free and are washed ashore, often during stormy weather. These kinds of fish lay eggs throughout the year, so hunting for egg-cases can be successful in any season, though spring and autumn are often best because this is when we tend to get the biggest storms.

This spring has seen some incredible storms. The photo above of Godrevy was taken a couple of weeks ago. Below is a view of Sennen and Gwynver Beach.

Today, Rory took us around the beach at Sennen, and we were lucky enough to find nine egg-cases of blonde rays; one of a small-eyed ray, and four of lesser-spotted catsharks. Identifying the fish by looking at its egg-case is a tricky business, and to be certain you need to soak the egg-case in water for several hours, which allows it to take on its natural size and colour, and then use the key, available on the Shark Trust website. Fortunately, it is relatively easy to pick out the egg-cases of the nursehound and lesser-spotted catshark, as these are both goblet-shaped and have long curly tendrils at each corner, though they do vary in colour from almost translucent to quite dark brown. The egg-cases of skates and rays are squarer in shape, and have variably shaped horns at their corners.

Though sharks and rays tend to be long-lived, they lay only a small number of eggs each year, so they are susceptible to over-fishing and even being caught accidentally as 'by-catch'. It is important that we gather information on where these creatures live and breed. One way to do this is to look for their egg-cases and report the findings to the Shark Trust, and that is why they are encouraging such egg hunts.

April 4th

A Date with a High Society

Since I write for *Cornwall Today*, you might expect me to be invited to plenty of high-society events. So when the Editor contacted me at the beginning of April to ask me to an engagement in Dobwalls, I was obviously thinking immediately of what I should wear: would a dinner jacket be appropriate, or should I dress down in a sports jacket and cravat? As it turned out, I needn't have worried about the DJ, because for this 'high society' event, I wouldn't be allowed in without steel toe-capped boots, a hard hat and a high-visibility jacket – much more my style!

The high society involved here were the bats that fly over the new Dobwalls bypass, but there were some important people including camera crews from the BBC and ITV. The reason for the interest was that two unusual bat bridges had been constructed across the new road. Apart from going to learn about the

The brown long-eared and noctule bats (top and above) are two of the many species that might benefit from the bat bridges over Dobwalls bypass.

bridges, I wanted to find out more about the ways in which new roads are built to minimize their impact on the environment.

Before the building of a new road can commence, surveys of the area are made to determine the least damaging route. These surveys take account of a variety of factors, including wildlife; archaeology; air quality for residents, and the visual effect of the road. Once a route has been established, work must be done to mitigate the negative impacts of the road against these criteria.

In terms of wildlife, careful studies along the route of the road are undertaken at different times of year. Attempts are made to capture and move protected species, such as reptiles and dormice, though few were found on the Dobwalls route. The type of animal possibly worst affected by this road is the bat. While surveying the site for bats, the wildlife specialists found two buildings and several trees which serve as roosts for at least four different species of bat (brown long-eared; pipistrelle; whiskered, and Brandt's). The buildings will be untouched by the work, but a couple of the trees would have to be removed. At a time of year when the bats were not roosting in the trees, the holes were blocked off to prevent them returning, so that the trees could be felled. To try to mitigate for this action, a special bat building was made for the bats to roost in. I'm not quite sure who is going to tell the bats, but it will be interesting to see if they make use of their new facility.

As well as having regular roost sites, bats also have regular flight paths. The same flight paths might well have been used for many years, and the bats remember their routes by memorizing the hedgerows along which they fly. The benefit of these regular routes is that the bats can find their way from their roost to areas of good feeding with minimal fuss. If we remove a hedgerow, it can cost the bats dearly: this will disrupt their routines, and might separate their roosts from areas of good feeding, leaving the bats to slowly decline. A large road might also split the bat population in two, possibly leaving traditional male roosts on one side and female roost sites on the other.

When constructing the Dobwalls bypass, three hedgerows that would have to be removed were found to be significant to the movement of bats. One was along a minor road which will now pass over the new bypass, and this has been adapted to be wider than is necessary, and to carry higher parapets to give the bats a more significant linear feature to navigate along safely. The other two hedges would not be replaced in such a straightforward fashion, and something unusual would have to be done to try to give the bats a safe route to follow above the dangerous and fast-moving traffic below. This is how the bat bridges came about.

A bat bridge is simply a structure at a safe height above the road which gives the bats something to fly along. Because they use echo-location to find their way around, they need something solid, like a hedgerow or bat bridge, to navigate along. These bat bridges are situated at approximately the same height as the hedgerows that were removed, and follow faithfully along the same lines. They consist of a metal framework cloaked in plastic mesh similar to a windbreak material. They have a U-shaped cross section, so, in theory, the bats could fly within the bridge, though it is far more likely that they will fly in the lee of it. Insects might congregate in their shelter, but they are primarily just a guide to encourage the bats safely across the road. I suppose you could say they are literally flyovers!

A bat bridge over the Dobwalls bypass (above), and the badger tunnel under the bypass, before being landscaped (below).

As you drive along the new bypass, look out for these bridges; they look like temporary gantries for signs, or possibly safety nets for erecting electric wires across the road. As you can imagine, making anything like this over a main road will have to meet stringent safety requirements, so isn't going to come cheap. In fact, the construction of these bridges came in at around £325,000. Is this money well spent, or is it money wasted in an attempt to appease conservationists? Well, the jury is out on that one for quite a few years.

Currently, only two other bat bridges have been built in Britain – one in Cumbria and one in Wales – and their success is not certain. We are still in the very early stages of this kind of work, and the bat bridges at Dobwalls are going to be used as

a piece of research to see if they can work. The Highways Agency will pay for the bats to be monitored here over at least the next five years, to see what effect the road has had on their population and activities. If it is successful, then further bat bridges might be springing up around the country; if it isn't, then they will need to be adapted.

The concept of providing safe routes for wildlife across our roads is not a new one, and many other species of wild animal have benefited from our concessions while building roads. One of the most successful of such ventures has been the badger underpass. This is simply a large pipe laid

under the road to allow badgers to pass freely and without danger. Like bats, badgers use the same pathways for many generations, and are reluctant to change their ways. Badger routes are now provided as standard, where appropriate, on new road builds.

Fish have also benefitted at Dobwalls, by the creation of a fish underpass complete with a ladder to allow them to swim upstream to their spawning grounds. One more creature which has had its own underpass created here is the otter. At the Liskeard end of the road, it passes over the East Looe River. Here there is regular activity among the otter population, a fact reinforced by the otter footprints recorded on a sheet of plastic laid out by the river. A culvert has been created to allow the river to pass under the road, but the flow of water in this culvert will be very strong at times, making life difficult for an otter passing upstream. Since the culvert has been increased in length, it would also create a very dark tunnel which would inhibit the movement of otters. To mitigate against this effect, two measures have been taken.

Otter footprints on a sheet of dirty plastic (top). Looking down through the light-well to the otter ledge (above).

First, a light-well has been opened up in the middle of the culvert. This is simply an opening in the ground to allow light into the culvert, and should make it more inviting to otters. Second, an otter ledge has been made to provide otters with the opportunity to walk through the culvert rather than swim. These measures are also now widely used on road-building schemes.

One thing that otters require more than anything else is fresh, clean water in which to find fish. A big new road with lots of cars on it will create a lot of pollutants, though it could be argued that if the volume of traffic does not increase the amount of pollution should decrease. This is especially true since new roads are all built with pollution-saving measures in place.

Cars are not 100 per cent efficient, so some of the fuel that the engines use is released from the exhaust pipe without being burnt up – a process known as incomplete combustion. This, along with other waste products resulting from our use of cars, leaves many pollutants including arsenic, copper, nickel and even asbestos on the road surface to be washed into the gutters at the side of the road. Measures are now built into all new road systems to remove these pollutants, allowing clean water to be released back into the natural water courses around the road.

For instance, here on the Dobwalls bypass there are three facilities for cleaning the polluted runoff from the road. The gutters carry water from the road into 'interceptor ponds'. These ponds are relatively small, but have reeds growing in them. The reeds purify the water, and the ponds have an overflow system to allow pure water to run out into

The attenuation pool and drainage from the road.

a large holding pond, known as an 'attenuation' pond. These attenuation ponds are large enough to cope with a major accident on the road such as the release of fuel from a large tanker. In this event, the fuel would flow into the pond where it could be safely removed and disposed of properly through a waste disposal mechanism. Assuming there is no major problem, the fresh water from the interceptor pond will gradually build up in the attenuation pond to a point where it can flow into the natural water course. At one point, the outflow of water has been taken over an area of ground where some shallow scrapes have also been dug. This will create new habitat for wetland plants such as ragged robin, meadowsweet and maybe marsh orchids, but only time will tell.

Another interesting measure to help wildlife and to minimize the visual impact of the road is found in the treatment of the roadside verges. The most obvious measure will be in the planting of trees; approximately 50,000 native trees will be planted along the Dobwalls bypass. The verges close to the road have already been seeded with grass, which is important for stabilizing the ground. Further from the road, and on the banks leading away from it, no topsoil has been added, and grass seed has been sown at a very low density to allow natural colonization of the ground by native flowering plants. It will be interesting to see which species grow here in future years.

April 21st

Soft Furnishings

Members of the tit family, like this great tit, have benefited from the provision of artificial nest sites in gardens.

Through April I have been working on a project to photograph birds gathering nesting material. Most of us enjoy watching birds feeding in our gardens, and that is partly why the bird-food industry has increased so much since it started at the end of the nineteenth century. I wouldn't mind betting that far fewer of us bother to support our garden birds when it comes to nest-building, but it is much more rewarding to watch a bird build a nest and raise its young than simply to watch it feed.

To encourage birds to nest in your garden, it is essential to provide a variety of suitable places for nest-building. Some birds, such as the blue tit, great tit and house sparrow, will take readily to nest boxes with a hole, even preferring them to 'natural' nest sites. In general, most birds prefer to find a place of their own, though the robin and spotted flycatcher will sometimes be tempted by an open-fronted nest box. One of the best spots for birds to nest is among ivy; this climber is evergreen, so provides thick protection, even in early spring. We have a pair of wrens, blackbirds, robins and song thrushes nesting in one clump of ivy growing against our garage. Some evergreen garden shrubs can also be very good for nesting birds, for the same reason.

Another general rule to promote the number of nesting birds in your garden is not to be too tidy. Over the last few weeks, I have watched birds collecting everything from dead grass, to old leaf skeletons, bits of twig, moss, lichen and feather to make their nests. If we kept our garden too tidy, the birds would have to travel further. I once weighed the contents of a great tit's nest and found that it was 80 grams; that doesn't sound much, but when you consider that a beak full of hair, or a feather, weigh a fraction of a gram, it soon becomes clear that Mr and Mrs Great Tit probably undertook about 800 sorties to gather that material.

A blue tit collecting spaniel hair (left). To get the photo on the right,
I cut all of our pampas grass and put out one piece at a time near the house.
(It saved the sparrow some air miles as well!).

Male birds don't always play a very active role in nest-building. The male wren has it tough, because he makes a choice of nests for his partner to choose from, and furbishes just one; but the male chiffchaff that I have been watching for the last few days has done little except sing and keep guard over his partner, while she has done all the work. I'm sure his whistling while she worked was greatly appreciated by his busy mate! The chiffchaff makes a ragged-looking nest from bits of grass, often quite low to the ground in a hedge, but 'my' pair has had the good sense to build under a substantial bramble leaf, which will serve as a roof.

In order that I could watch birds gathering their nesting material, I deliberately set out to provide them with the materials they might need. I started by collecting together some useful resources such as wool, hair and pampas grass to dispense in our garden. The hair, from my dog as well as myself, I put in an old peanut feeder which I hung among the other bird feeders where the birds were accustomed to visiting. I put some sheep's wool in another dispenser which was designed for containing fat balls, as well as attaching some to photogenic pieces of barbed wire and bramble around the garden. I gathered some whole heads of pampas grass and secured them in position near where the house sparrows nest, thus enabling me to watch their activities closely.

The birds that took advantage of my hospitality were the great tits and blue tits, which are nesting in nest boxes in the garden; they took only the dog's hair from the peanut dispenser. The goldfinches, which are always

*The chiffchaff (above) found its own nest site and its own nesting material.
A swallow (below) collects mud and straw for nest-building.*

plentiful in our garden, have been messing about with the wool but haven't yet really got a grasp of the need to make nests. The house sparrows have been ripping the pampas grass to pieces, as they will continue to do throughout the year; their nests are a massive mess of nesting material crammed into their boxes, leaving only a tiny space for eggs and young. I often think that house sparrows have a psychological problem, causing them to compulsively build nests, and they don't know when to stop.

Birds' nests are often amazing constructions; the nest of a long-tailed tit is made of spiders' webs and lichens.

The robin and chiffchaff haven't made use of my nesting material, but have found plenty without my help. Meanwhile, just returned from Africa, the swallows which make their homes in our garage are already showing signs of refurbishing their old nests. The pig's wallow in our top field is always a great place to see them collecting mud and straw to create their nest masterpieces.

By watching the birds collecting material, it is also quite a simple task to spot where they are nesting. Follow their regular path and they will guide you to their nest. I would never tamper with a nest to get a better view, because it can lead to the young birds being predated, but if we know where the birds are nesting we are better placed to ensure their success by avoiding too much gardening work in that area... now there's a good excuse!

The goldfinches have been examining our sheep's wool, but not really collecting it with gusto.

A Scilly Holiday

On St Agnes, this is my natural diet: sticky toffee pudding and locally made ice-cream.

I didn't mention in March that Sarah and I had a week-long break on the Isles of Scilly. For that trip we stayed on Bryher, and were delighted by stormy weather that hit Hell Bay while we were there. The main driving force behind that trip, and, to some extent, this one, was to take photos of the islands for a book which will have been published long before you read this one. However, the main reason for going to Scilly in May, rather than chasing storms, was to photograph wildlife, and especially to seek out spring flowers around the coast of the islands.

The Scillies are renowned among ornithologists for their ability to attract rare migrants; this is true of both spring and autumn, although it is the latter period which has the greatest potential for mega-rarities. Even so, I managed to see a bee-eater and a red-rumped swallow, as well as many slightly less rare birds during our stay. In fact, I won't be forgiven if I don't admit that it was Sarah who first spotted the red-rumped swallow: it was only a matter of a split second before I saw it, and I'm not bitter at all!

I enjoy seeing rare birds, particularly if I find them myself; but they are nothing more than the candles on top of a cake: they give you a spark of light and something to remember, but the cake tastes just as good without them. The Scilly cake is full of goodies, and a holiday on the islands is just about as relaxing as a holiday can get.

We spent the first three days on St Agnes, partaking regularly of the sticky toffee pudding of Covean café. We were serenaded by cuckoos on Wingletang; cuckolded by lesser black-backed gulls on Gugh, and befriended by song thrushes all around the island. So common and so

A storm hits Hell Bay, Bryher, earlier in the year (right).

A song thrush tucking into its natural diet – a snail (above). A lesser black-backed gull on Gugh (below), and a kitttiwake (bottom), which breeds on the islands. The tidal bar to Gugh from St Agnes (left).

tame do some individuals become that they insist on sitting at your table to eat cake from your plate.

I spent many happy hours following song thrushes around, trying to photograph them eating a more natural diet. Here there are snails aplenty, and the song thrush likes nothing more than to grab a snail and bash it against a rock until its shell succumbs, which is usually after the first sharp blow.

The subsequent seven days were spent on St Mary's, from where we travelled to off-islands and took boat trips to see the seals and seabirds. There are many different seabirds nesting around Scilly, including: cormorant; shag; common tern; kittiwake; gulls (lesser black-backed, great black-backed and herring); Manx shear-water; storm petrel; guillemot,

*Typical Scilly scenery: Watermill Cove, St Mary's (above).
Cromwell's Castle, Tresco (below).*

razorbill and puffin. Of all of these, the puffin is the star. To see puffins it is necessary to take a boat trip. The boatmen of St Mary's take trips to various remote parts of the islands, and they know where the puffins are to be found. For me, it was a trip around Annet that came up trumps.

Despite having travelled to the islands many times in the last twenty years, this was the first trip on which I managed to get across to the uninhabited island of Samson. This episode required a boat-to-rubber-dinghy transfer in the middle of the sea and a paddle at the other end, but even that experience was surpassed by our visit to White Island.

White Island is a tidal island connected to St Martin's at low tide by a rocky bar. We had been to this small island many times, but never

Thrift in flower on White Island (above). Puffins are one of the biggest attractions for the nature-loving visitor to the islands (below).

in May, and there was one special reason for going there: thrift. The last time we went, in September, I noticed that on the extreme parts of White Island there was an incredible amount of thrift. In September it wasn't in flower, but the characteristic pillow-shaped mounds of this plant gave me enough confidence to plan our whole holiday around coming back to see this thrift in flower in the middle of May.

From St Martin's we could see nothing that made us confident about my anticipated floral spectacular, so it was with some trepidation that we walked across the difficult rocky bar to White Island. It wasn't until we rounded the corner at the northern edge of the island that my wish came true. You can have the candle; the song thrush can have the cake; this was the icing! I have never seen thrift growing like this before, and probably never shall again. I am not aware of anywhere else in Cornwall that comes close to this, and I have seen some other stunningly impressive collections of this pretty flower. Set against a blue sky, with Round Island lighthouse sitting in a turquoise sea, this could be heaven.

May 25th

Up at Dawn, Asleep by Midday

We returned from Scilly on Saturday 24 May. The forecast for the following day was about as poor as it could be, which was a shame because I had booked to go on a dawn chorus walk from Respryn Bridge near Lanhydrock. Mind you, it isn't ever really possible to rely on weather forecasts for Cornwall, since most television forecasters stand in front of our county to talk of Wiltshire, Gloucestershire and Dorset as being 'in the South West'!

Having just returned from holiday, I had a pile of letters, phone messages and emails that would take me several days to plough through, so the idea of getting up before dawn to go walking in the pouring rain didn't fill me with enthusiasm. However, there were two reasons why I couldn't back out. One was that I really wanted to do a dawn chorus, but had been putting it off all through the early part of May, and this was the last organized walk that I knew of. The other was that, later in the same morning, I was due to go and help out on a dormouse survey in a CWT nature reserve very close to Lanhydrock. This survey date had been arranged around me, and because I had been on Scilly it had to be today.

Sarah was a bit unkind: knowing that I was tired and a little reluctant to get up early, she asked, 'Do birds sing in torrential rain, then?', as she set the alarm for 4.15 a.m. I should have been more careful in my planning; I hadn't noticed that this was a bank holiday weekend. What better guarantee of bad weather could there be?

As always, when the alarm is set, I woke up about half an hour before it went off. As I put the dog out I could hear the rain falling on the porch roof, and despite the dog running straight back in I took heart from the fact that she wasn't completely drenched. The drive to Lanhydrock takes about an hour, and during that time the rainfall became gradually heavier. I arrived at about 5.45 a.m., in good time for our 6 a.m. start, which is actually about an hour after dawn, though it was still as dark as night on this particular occasion.

The location of our dawn chorus: Lanhydrock in May (right), but not this May!

Nuthatch (above) and great spotted woodpecker (below) were two of the species we heard as the rain stopped and we headed back to our cars.

I was amazed to see not only Sid Cole, the walk leader, but also another couple who were mad enough to come along just for the pleasure. I hadn't met Sid before, but he is an experienced walk leader and an extremely dedicated birder, taking part in ornithological surveys including monitoring of the recently released cirl buntings in Cornwall.

This morning would prove to be a challenge for him, though. When we paused to listen for birdsong, the sound of the wind in the trees and the rain falling on our hats and waterproofs was enough to drown out the song of any bird brave enough to step into the limelight. As Sid pointed out, the truth is that by the end of May most resident birds will have stopped singing. The main reasons for birds to sing are to attract a mate and maintain a territory, and by the end of May even the summer migrants will mostly have found partners. The bad weather was enough to stop nearly all of the remaining single males from bursting forth into song… but not all of them.

Grey wagtails (above) are common along the River Fowey at Respryn.
A redstart (below) was the best find of our dawn chorus walk.

Despite the atrocious weather, we had heard several common species before we paused to listen carefully to the song of a bird at the top of an oak tree. There was no way we could hope to see this bird – the foliage was far too thick for us to get a view, and if we looked up through binoculars our lenses would immediately be covered in raindrops – but Sid quickly identified it as a redstart, a quite uncommon bird at Lanhydrock. He made a recording of the song on his digital voice recorder. This inexpensive device enabled him to record any birdsongs that he heard for his own enjoyment, and would allow less experienced birdwatchers to identify birds by recording their song and asking an expert. (A very good idea, and one which would prove to be important for my own experiences later in the year.)

This identification process demonstrated perfectly to me the value of such a guided walk. Not only did we force ourselves to listen to every birdsong, but, with the help of our leader, we also identified each one. It is so much easier in a woodland setting to hear a bird than it is to see one, but learning birdsong can be daunting to many people. This is an ideal way to learn a new skill.

A dormouse in torpor (left). Jenny Stuart weighs a dormouse (right).

Fortunately, the rain did abate a little at around 7.30 a.m., when we actually saw some birds, including spotted flycatchers as well as nuthatch, great spotted woodpecker, grey wagtail, and a variety of tits and warblers, on the return to our cars.

A dawn chorus can be a fantastic, quite moving experience; this morning had been a little less spectacle and more struggle, but still better than lying in bed! Next year I will get out at the beginning of May for a dawn chorus walk, and I won't go if the forecast includes the word 'torrential'!

I wondered how dormice respond to freezing cold wet weather in May. Well, I was about to find out. A short drive from Lanhydrock, under the peak of Helman Tor, is the nature reserve of Redmoor. Here, the CWT has erected about 100 nest boxes specifically for dormice, monitoring them monthly throughout the summer months for the last few years.

I met up with Jenny Stuart, who works for Cornwall Environmental Consultants (CEC), a company associated with CWT, which, among other things, undertakes survey work of natural history on sites earmarked for possible development. Jenny is a licensed dormouse handler. You might not know this, but it is a criminal act to interfere with a dormouse in any way unless you have a licence or can prove that your actions were intended to protect the creature from impending harm. So even if you put up nest boxes for them on your own land, it is an offence to look in the boxes if you expect dormice to be in there.

A dormouse in the hand (above) is worth going out for on a wet day!

Seeing a dormouse in the wild demands either great patience or very good fortune. It is likely that they are quite widespread across Cornwall, but they are probably most common in the east of the county.

I was surprised to learn that dormice don't emerge from hibernation until May – possibly the end of April, but definitely no earlier. Unlike other species which hibernate, the dormouse has difficulty in finding food until May, when insects, buds and blossoms are more numerous. For this reason, the tiny dormouse has to put on a lot of weight in the autumn before disappearing underground to spend the winter in a deep sleep.

When it emerges from hibernation in May, its first job is to construct a nest, or at least to find somewhere safe and dry to sleep. The nest of a dormouse is typically built from woven strips of honeysuckle bark; into this it knits freshly plucked leaves of hazel and bits of moss, all of which are collected from the branches of trees where it will spend the entire summer. A nest box, with its hole pressed not so tightly against the trunk of a tree, is a great place for a dormouse to seek refuge.

The breeding season is short for dormice. Unlike wood mice, for example, which can have several litters each year, the dormouse often has just one, or occasionally two. Each litter may have between four and six young, but to compensate for this low productivity, the dormouse can live a long life of up to five years, whereas the wood mouse is lucky to see its first birthday.

We set about tracking through the woodland, looking for the numbered boxes, and for the first ten or so found nothing but a family of blue

A dormouse nest (left) is generally made from strips of honeysuckle bark and freshly cut leaves.

You can identify the creature from an eaten hazel nut (right). A dormouse has left tooth marks on the outside of the shell at an angle to the edge of the hole.

tits whose parents had squeezed in through the hole pressed close to the tree trunk; mother was a little alarmed by our intrusion, but surprisingly sat tight on her clutch of eggs. As we entered the denser part of the woodland, we had our first success: a pair of dormice, one male and one female, were fast asleep together. The male was much heavier than the female, and they had already started to weave a new nest.

The cold, wet weather had meant that they were not likely to have been out feeding for many hours, so they were doing what dormice do best! The 'dor' of dormouse comes from the French word *dormir*, which means 'to sleep'. In fact, dormice don't sleep like we do, but enter a state of torpor, somewhere between sleeping and hibernating. Their metabolic rate drops very low, to conserve energy, and when they are found and handled they just continue sleeping, apparently unaware of the intrusion.

Even so, they need to be handled carefully and quickly to avoid waking them. Jenny weighed each one and sexed them, if she could, without causing any discomfort to the mouse! She jotted down the details she needed, before replacing the mice and moving on. Of the 100 boxes, about ten contained dormice, usually in pairs and almost all in torpor. Of the other boxes, there were three that had the nests of blue or great tits, and the rest were empty except for a rather intimidating buzzing sound from one which we decided to pass over! This was in stark contrast to the last dormouse survey in which I took part during a spell of sunny weather, when most of the boxes seemed to contain wood mice and all of the dormice we found were alert and rather active.

So the wet weather might have spoilt my dawn chorus, but at least it meant that I was able to see and photograph dormice. These amazing creatures in their curled up torpid position are about as cute as our wildlife can get. Seeing them at close quarters is a real privilege.

June 3rd

Clovers at the Drop of a Hat

It is said that in 1847, the botanist the Revd C.A. Johns of Helston, found so many rare clovers on one sloping hillside at Caerthillian Cove on the Lizard that he was able to cover eight different species with his hat! The Revd Johns was a teacher at Helston Grammar School as well as a distinguished botanist. He published several books, including *A Week at The Lizard* (1848), which described the clovers at Caerthillian, and *Flowers of the Field*, which was an important nineteenth-century field guide. What I wanted to investigate was whether Caerthillian is a remarkable place for clovers, or whether they had particularly big hats in the nineteenth century.

Not being very experienced at identifying rare clovers, I decided that I would need the help of an expert, so I recruited Dr Colin French. Colin is a self-employed

Clovers at the drop of a hat. Colin French searches for clovers at Caerthillian.

ecological consultant, specializing in botany. He spends a great deal of time working voluntarily to map the plants of Cornwall and, with the help of many other volunteers belonging to the Botanical Cornwall Group, has created a massive database of records known as ERICA.

Before venturing out, Colin explained to me that we were unlikely to find as many species of clover as recorded by the Revd Johns. Of the

Clockwise from top left: Twin-flowered clover with a single flower head.
Knotted clover with a twin-flowered head... confused? An upright clover...
at least it was upright! The bog-standard white clover is much larger than the
rarer varieties found at Caerthillian – here it is seen growing with bird's foot
trefoil. Burrowing clover was one of the five species under my hat.

twelve species ever recorded on the famous slope within Caerthillian Cove, recent surveys had revealed only seven or eight. These surveys were often carried out by teams of people on field meetings, so what chance would Colin and I have of dropping a hat on eight species? We did have one unfair advantage over the Revd Johns, though, and that came in the form of the 'western clover', which grows in the area and was first recognized

Shetland ponies graze at Caerthillian during the winter.

as being a different species from the bog-standard 'white clover' only in 1950, so Johns wouldn't have had that one on his list!

My first personal problem would be in interpreting my guide! Being of a botanical background, Colin would insist on referring to all plants by their scientific name – indeed, even claiming that he didn't know their common names. I, however, being of a non-specialist background, can only remember common names. Fortunately, I had taken along my trusty field guide to the flowers of Britain and Europe, so was able to translate. Unfortunately, that was the limit of the usefulness of my field guide because, even though all of the clovers were listed, described and illustrated, it was pretty useless at helping to identify them. Colin had prepared a key which he painstakingly used to separate out the different species.

Leaf shape; extent of hairs or down; shape and colour of stipules; colour of flower, and many other points were used, along with a hand lens to pick out the key distinguishing details... and that is when you have found a clover! This difficulty was highlighted by the identification of the twin-flowered clover, *Trifolium bocconei*. In my wildflower guide, the only feature given for this species to distinguish it from the very similar knotted clover is that it 'often' has paired flowers. The first example of the twin-flowered clover that we found had just one head, and Colin could only identify it because its leaves were hairy on the underside only, and they had a purple edge to their tips.

The view along the rugged coastline from Caerthillian Cove.

As the morning progressed, I began to feel a bit useless. Colin would track down these tiny plants by methodically and meticulously scrutinizing the area. He would then identify, record and plot them on his GPS, before pointing them out to me and moving on. It then took me the time it would take him to find the next one to get some photos of the last one! I hope it is my care and attention to photographic detail rather than my inability to spot flowers that led to Colin finding the lion's share of the clovers! The grass and other flowers on this slope are quite short, so you might think it would be a simple task to find clovers, but it isn't. The flowers of the rarer clovers are very small, and it is unusual to find them in full colour, so Colin would base his identification on flower heads that had gone to seed, or those that hadn't yet fully emerged.

'We' did exceptionally well to find an amazing ten species of clover on this one slope, along with some others in the wider area. I took the biggest hat I owned and, while Colin was looking for more flowers, tried placing it to cover as many clovers as possible. The largest number I managed to drop my hat on was only five, so I must take my hat off to the Revd Johns; but given our expectations of the day, I think we did incredibly well.

If you don't believe how difficult it is to identify clovers, then may I suggest that you try it for yourself? The best time to pay a visit to Caerthillian is at the end of May or beginning of June. All the details you will need are in the Appendix (page 188), and the photos on page 76 will get you started. Good luck!

June 7th

Moonlit Flit

There is a bewildering array of days and weeks set aside in our calendar to celebrate or promote unusual causes. For instance, this year, on 22 February we were encouraged to take part in a 'work your proper hours day' – the purpose of which was to only work for the hours that you are paid (thank goodness my wife hasn't heard of that one!). The 'real nappy week' probably needs no explanation and is a very good cause, but not one that I want to think about too much. I love the idea of 'compost awareness week' from 4 to 10 May; it makes me think of people with woolly hats all over the country sitting by their compost bins, spending quality time with their compost. The following week is when the rest of humanity indulges itself in 'national doughnut week'. 'Be nice to nettles week', from 14 to 25 May is obviously organized by someone who can't count, and though I sympathize with their passion I can't help but think

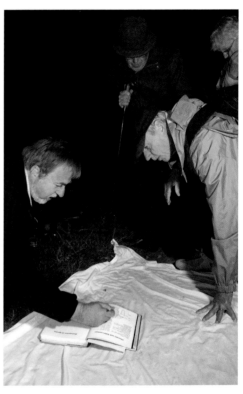

Phil Boggis explains how to identify a green carpet moth on a white sheet.

that there are probably enough nettles in the countryside already, and even when I shout abuse at the nettles in my garden they still grow well enough anyway.

Enough of that. 7 June is not an obscure national day, it is 'National Moth Night', and if you are wondering who on earth came up with this idea, then I can tell you, it was conceived in Cornwall by Mark Tunmore,

Clockwise from top left: A pale tussock moth resting on my finger.
The peppered moth, a master of disguise. One of the most colourful moths
attracted is known as the brimstone. A scalloped hazel moth, which landed
on the white sheet.

who is the editor of *Atropos*, a national journal focusing on butterflies, moths and dragonflies. National Moth Night, now in its tenth year, is currently organized by *Atropos* (which is part of the scientific name of the death's-head hawkmoth) in association with Butterfly Conservation. They even have prizes for those who make the most records, or see the rarest moths, etc.

National Moth Night is intended to encourage the wider public to become involved in an area of our natural history that has attracted little interest in the past. Influxes of the hummingbird hawkmoth into Cornwall each summer are the limit of the media's interest in this subject, but with around 2,500 species of moth in Britain, many of which are colourful and unusual, there is a great deal of interest and a lot to learn. It is also hoped that surveyors taking part in National Moth Night will be able to collect some valuable data that will serve a scientific purpose. To this end, Butterfly Conservation is currently leading a large partnership of surveyors and funders in a four-year project to establish a national moth-recording scheme, the focus of which will be the 900 or so macro moths (larger species) found in the UK.

The date of National Moth Night changes annually, so that different species can be targeted each year. The tenth anniversary saw the introduction of some daytime moth events, such as one at Windmill Farm on the Lizard, but I opted to attend a more traditional event at dusk, on the summit of Kit Hill, near Callington.

Kit Hill is owned by Cornwall Council (CC), and a wide range of events is organized there. This one was led by Phil Boggis, a moth specialist. To attract the moths, he brought along a mercury vapour lamp, powered by a portable generator. The lamp stood about 1 metre high, and underneath it he placed a white sheet on the ground... well, it was white until three dogs decided to run across it as he was setting up.

Phil started by telling us that we probably wouldn't see many moths tonight. (This is a strategy which I find many people adopt when leading guided events, because it lowers the expectations of the audience – a wise move!) However, he went on to qualify that statement by explaining about weather conditions and how that affects moths. First, it was

If the moths we saw tonight aren't impressive enough to grab you, what about the poplar hawkmoth for size (top), or the buff-tip moth for camouflage (above)?

a clear night, and that isn't ideal. Even though there was only a small sliver of a moon, this would create enough light to make the moths nervous of being caught by bats. It was quite calm, but the breeze on top of the hill wasn't ideal for moths, so he had set up at the top of a gulley near the old quarry.

Once the sun had set, moths slowly started to appear, and, attracted by the ultra-violet light of the mercury vapour lamp, many flapped around the light before dropping down on to the white sheet. Phil caught them in clear plastic pots to identify them, and then passed them around the assembled audience. Obviously, it helps to have an expert at hand. It might have taken the rest of us many hours to pick out each of these moths from the 900 featured in one of his guidebooks. On top of those, there are the even more numerous smaller species, some of which even Phil had some difficulty with.

The fact that many of these species are difficult to identify shouldn't stop us taking part in moth-watching. Many species are impressive and colourful. Moths are covered in tiny scales, which give them their wonderful and varied colours and patterns. In fact, it is these scales that are responsible for the scientific name for moths, *Lepidoptera*, which originates from the Greek word *lepido*, meaning 'scales'. These scales are easily removed, and older moths may look nothing like the fresh individuals that are replicated in guidebooks. It's almost like trying to identify birds without any feathers. Fresher individuals can be remarkably attractive, and some are easy to identify; it's just a matter of starting with the commonest and building up a wider knowledge.

Sarah and I stayed for two hours, from 9.30 p.m. to 11.30 p.m., in which time we saw at least nineteen different species of moth, and had a cup of warming soup, provided by CC. If you don't want to get involved in this way, then try leaving an outside light on at home for the evening, and see what is attracted to it; or leave the curtains open and see which moths are attracted to your window. One thing is for sure, you will be eaten by fewer midges doing it this way, and I don't know that wearing insect repellent is quite the right approach for a moth night; but I didn't tell that to the lady who slapped the side of her face when a moth accidentally landed there!

June 10th

Bats in the Belfry

As far as moths are concerned, bats are enemy number one, so after National Moth Night I thought it was time to catch up with some of our more interesting bats. To do so, I met up with Jane Squirrell, who is Species Officer for Natural England covering Devon, Cornwall and the Isles of Scilly. This title sounds a bit expansive, but Jane's efforts are concentrated on the more endangered varieties of wildlife, such as dormice and bats. For today we would be looking for greater horseshoe bats, a rare and endangered species found at a small number of locations in Cornwall.

At Jane's recommendation, we met at Creed Church in the early evening. When I arrived, Jane was chatting with the church caretaker, Stella Thomas. Stella held the key to the part of the church buildings in which there is often a roost of greater

Creed Church.

horseshoe bats. We entered the building quietly, to avoid disturbing the bats, but were a little disappointed to find only one greater horseshoe, which was rather active and quickly left the building.

The pile of droppings on the floor didn't look promising. Jane had a close look, and explained that most of it didn't look very fresh, indicating that not many bats had been using this roost recently. Looking at bat muck might not sound a very exciting hobby, but this practice has proved very useful to ecologists over the last few years. It is only through close

Greater horseshoe bats huddle together in their maternity roost.

inspection of their droppings that we have learned exactly what the bats eat at various times of the year. The droppings comprise largely of insect exoskeletons, often the shiny black wing-cases of beetles, and by examining these we can now be sure that in May greater horseshoe bats eat a lot of cockchafers, and during the summer they are partial to dung beetles.

Before we go any further, I should explain that greater horseshoe bats use a variety of different roost sites through the year, and each has a different purpose. Over winter they have roost sites known as 'hibernacula', because it is here that they hibernate. For the greater horseshoes in the Creed area, it is this stage of their annual cycle about which we know least. There may well be roosts in the area that we just don't know about, maybe in old mining adits. The nearest known hibernacula for this species of bat is around St Agnes, and it seems inconceivable that these bats could fly all that way to hibernate.

After emerging from hibernation in the spring, the bats get together at 'gathering roosts'. This is usually when Creed Church is used, but this year it looks like they have found somewhere else. After this period they will split into single-sex groups, with males going to bachelor roosts and females attending maternity roosts to give birth, normally in July. Once the young are old enough, the bats will gather together again, which is when they mate, before going back to hibernation in the autumn.

Though mating takes places in late summer, the female bats hold the sperm inside them, delaying fertilization of the egg, so that the birth can take place the following summer. They can even delay the development of the young bat if conditions are unsuitable. Greater horseshoes give birth to just one young bat every two or three years, but to compensate for this low productivity they can live for between 20 and 30 years.

Greater horseshoe bats are quite fussy in their requirements, in terms of both diet and roost site. Unlike most bats, they like to fly around inside their roosts in order to 'test the light', particularly around dusk. They also fly direct to the place in which they will literally hang out for the daytime, whereas most bats land and crawl into a small crack or hole. For this reason, they need a large roost site with a lot of headroom.

To discuss their dietary requirements in a little more detail, Jane took me to the top of Creed Church tower. That in itself was an interesting experience. I thought the spiral staircase was a bit tight until I reached the ladder, but even that had nothing on

A greater horseshoe bat grooming.

the small access hole on to the roof. From the top we had a great view of the surrounding landscape, and could readily see the types of farming employed here. The critical feature for greater horseshoes is that there are plenty of cattle in the fields; not only are there plenty of cattle, but many of the farmers in this area have converted, or are converting, to organic methods.

Cattle are important because where there are cows there is dung, and with dung come beetles, which the bats love. The only potential problem in this equation is the use of chemicals to worm the cattle; some chemicals can make the dung sterile, but on organic farms this is not a problem. In return for their organic status, farmers can be rewarded with extra funding for managing their land, through schemes such as Higher Level Stewardship.

The other feature of the landscape around Creed which is helpful to the bats is the small field systems and good-quality hedgerows, both of which bats find productive for hunting over. It is particularly important that there is good feeding for bats around their maternity roost, since mother bats cannot afford to waste energy flying a long way to hunt at such a critical time, when they are lactating. Jane explained that, within Cornwall, the biggest maternity roost for the greater horseshoe bats – with

Jane Squirrell and Stella Thomas stand at the entrance to the bats' gathering roost (left).

The view from Creed Church tower, showing good bat habitat with good hedgerows and cattle (right).

about 300 bats – is at Minster Church, near Boscastle, and the second biggest is near to Creed. That is where we would make for next, but Jane made it clear that the exact location of this maternity roost must remain a secret. Don't get me wrong, she didn't blindfold me, and tie me up in the boot of her car, but I can't divulge the information here.

The maternity roost site is in an old barn. Unfortunately, this barn is becoming a bit old and decayed for its purpose. The roof has some gaps, and the upstairs floor is starting to fall through. You might think that this would be ideal for bats, but it isn't. Mothers need to keep their young at a fairly constant 22°C, otherwise the likelihood of them dying in infancy increases significantly. Since this species of bat is heavily protected, it is an offence to disturb one of its roosts, so it is illegal for the owner of the barn to destroy it, but this barn is essentially being left to decay, despite money being offered to manage its upkeep. In time, this building will become unsuitable for the bats, and they will have to find an alternative roost site.

Jane has been discussing the options with many local landowners, and at present has two possibilities. The better of the two appears to be to the south of this location, where a family is developing a building and wishes to create a barn roost site especially for the bats. If this comes about, then the bats really couldn't ask for any more!

Back at the old barn, it was time to have a closer look at who was in residence. What followed was a defining moment in my bat-watching experience. We parted the honeysuckle and ivy that had been growing undisturbed over the doorway for what looked like the last few years, and, as quietly as we could, lifted the latch to the top half of the old, peeling barn door. Slowly we pushed back both halves of the door, before treading carefully on to the rotting floorboards of the first storey of this barn.

Peeping around the door we could see groups of bats hanging from the joists at the top of the barn. Some were hanging by themselves, and others were huddled in groups for warmth. Only a very few of them were motionless; the rest were in various stages of activity, which ranged from spinning around to flying around, or jostling for position in their tight clusters. Jane told me that if you watch carefully you can see that the bats change positions like emperor penguins in the Antarctic, so that each one takes its turn on the outside of the pack.

We didn't have long to count them and take a photo, but before we left I also wanted to make a sound recording of their voices. I had never before seen a greater horseshoe bat in the wild, let alone listened to one, so I had taken along a bat detector and my new digital voice recorder on which to record the sounds they made. These sounds are inaudible to the human ear because of the high frequency at which they are transmitted, but a bat detector lowers the frequency into a range that we can hear. I have heard that the sound of a greater horseshoe bat can be likened to a warbling, but no description can ever prepare you for the real thing. I can say quite safely that this is one of the strangest sounds I have ever heard in nature; it is right up there on the weird scale with the Manx shearwater, but at the same time is quite compelling. Think of the Sirens of Greek mythology appearing in an episode of Star Trek, and you won't be far from the sound of a greater horseshoe bat.

I use the term 'voice' a little loosely when referring to the horseshoe bats. This species of bat actually emits its echo-locating sounds through its nostrils, and uses its nose flap to vary them. The characteristic horseshoe-shaped nose-leaf of this bat is used to direct the sounds into a 'beam', which means that it can only echo-locate ahead of itself, unlike most bats which use a 'surround-sound' version of echo-location.

On close inspection, we could count about 100 bats in the roost – a good number for this time of year. It is still early for bats to be in their maternity roost, so hopefully the number will increase further over the next few weeks.

June 11th

The Rule of Bird-Surveying

When undertaking a bird survey, it is important to be able to identify birds, such as this song thrush, by their songs.

In January I wrote about the difference between birders and twitchers, and now it is time to take a closer look at one aspect of a birder's life. The birder in question is Martin Rule, who lives near Helston. Martin once worked for the Environment Agency, but left to establish his own business as an ecological consultant; he also undertakes practical conservation work, as well as filling in with a bit of gardening, but you can bet your life that he is always looking for ways to improve the environment for wildlife.

Martin is most definitely not a twitcher, and though he is naturally restrained in his views, it is clear that he feels birdwatchers should undertake more survey work and less rarity-seeking. It is only through regular and organized surveying that we can track changes in the populations of birds. How else would we be able to measure the current dramatic decline in the house sparrow and starling, for example?

One of the most important surveys undertaken in Britain, the Breeding Bird Survey, is jointly organized by the British Trust for Ornithology (BTO),

Martin Rule regularly leads guided walks for a number of charities, including the Helford Voluntary Marine Conservation Group and CWT.

the RSPB, and the Joint Nature Conservation Committee. One of its main uses has been to establish lists of breeding species that are threatened in the UK (see Appendix, page 189). Its success depends greatly on the network of volunteers established through the BTO. The UK is split into 124 regions, each of which has a regional organizer who is responsible for assigning survey squares to volunteers.

The squares correspond to 1 km grid squares on the Ordnance Survey maps, and these are pre-selected by the BTO across the country to randomly cover a variety of habitats and areas. Effectively, this means that a volunteer cannot choose their own square, because this would lead to biased data. It is likely that most people would choose areas that had a high potential for discovering birds, but it is important that all different types of squares are covered.

So if volunteers put their name forward, they will be given a square as close as possible to them. Martin has been taking part in this survey for thirteen years, and he is responsible for SW6833 – hardly a romantic name, but this is the four-figure grid reference of the square containing Porkellis Bridge, just to the north of Helston.

The first job for the volunteer is to establish two transects that cross the square, either east to west or north to south. A transect is simply a straightish line using footpaths, lanes or tracks, and if the square has been surveyed before this information will be provided. Each transect is

The stock dove was a new tick for Martin in his survey area.

split into five equal parts, and the surveyor simply looks for birds from each part. Then the habitat along the transects is recorded to allow birds to be matched to habitat.

Since this is a statistical survey, there are a number of rules to follow. For instance, each volunteer must undertake two birdwatching surveys during the breeding season: one around the end of April, and the other around early June. Each survey should ideally start between 6 a.m. and 7 a.m. Martin reckons that his survey lasts about 90 minutes, because you are expected to walk slowly but steadily, stopping only to identify birds and their song. It is best to be consistent from year to year, in terms of the time of start and weather conditions; in fact, surveying during the rain is discouraged because, as we already know, birds don't sing in wet weather.

Some experience is necessary to do this work justice, because most of the birds, particularly in early June when the trees have leaves, will only be identified by song. Martin thinks the most frequently observed bird in his survey area is the wren, with about eight regularly found along one transect, but few of these are actually seen.

A recording form is provided for volunteers, which enables the species to be recorded in such a way that the approximate distance of the bird from the transect line can be determined, or even if the bird was flying overhead. This data is then transferred to a summary sheet which is sent to the Regional Organizer.

All in all, this is not a huge amount of time or effort, and it is rewarding to take part in a national survey which helps to monitor our breeding-bird

In Martin's survey area, it is the yellowhammer that has declined more than any other bird.

population. There is another level of satisfaction to this work as well, and that is on a more personal level. Being an ex-Mathematics teacher, I am always interested by statistics, and to build up a personal bank of meaningful statistics for one area year after year is quite fascinating. Taking part in the BTO Breeding Bird Survey provides the discipline required to get up early twice a year and do just that.

If you don't feel able to take part in such a survey, it can be just as satisfying to organize your own. It might be that you walk a path near your home regularly, or just have time to sit and watch birds in your garden. Devise a set of rules by which your survey will work, and apply those over the next few years. Put the results on to a computer, and in a few years time you will be able to look back and spot trends.

Despite Martin having walked this route twice each spring for the last thirteen years, when he took me along to show me how he fulfils the survey, we discovered a new bird for 'his' square: a stock dove. This isn't a mega-rarity, nor is it particularly exciting, but it provided a bit of a buzz for Martin, even though he was a little annoyed that this wouldn't make it on to his survey records because he had completed that last week! I guess this helps to highlight the difference between a birder and a twitcher.

June 17th

A Sea Safari

The Orca Sea Safaris boat.

It is a few years since Orca Sea Safaris commenced operations from Falmouth. With a big powerful rigid inflatable boat (RIB), and fairly expensive prices, I wondered how they would ever find enough wildlife to keep enticing people to go out on trips. Well, the boat is still running, albeit under different management, and yet I had never been on one of their trips until today. So what was it like?

I chose to go today because last week there had been the biggest stranding of dolphins ever experienced in Cornwall. Twenty-six were found dead, and many more were helped back out to sea when a large number of common dolphins found their way into Carrick Roads. Speculation as to the cause of this sad event included some suspicion of the Navy, who were using sonar and firing weapons in the area at the time; it might have been that this coincided with a significant movement of dolphins, and that they were scared into the Roads; but this remains only a theory.

To my dismay, Matt Mcleod, skipper of the RIB, informed us that before the strandings there had been a few dolphins and several basking sharks in the area, but since then there had been none. Shark sightings are directly linked to the availability of plankton, whereas dolphins feed on fish, which in turn depend upon plankton. Fish will often gather together in a bubbling mass at the surface of the sea, and seabirds, such

Grey seals on Black Rock, with Pendennis Castle in the distance (above).
Gannets are seen frequently from the boat (below).

as gannets, will be seen in flocks feeding on these fish. It is these signs that Matt looks for when taking out groups of people in the RIB. Alas, for us today, there were no fish balls, not many gannets, and no dolphins or basking sharks.

Given that I really wanted to see dolphins, it would be reasonable to think that I came back from the trip a little dismayed and downhearted, but that isn't the case. We did see interesting wildlife and enjoyed a great trip. I guess the wildlife that we saw was the standard fare, but to describe a close-up view of grey seals hauled out on Black Rock just off Pendennis Castle as 'standard fare' would be a little unkind and very narrow-

Guillemots line up along a ledge on Gull Rock (above).
  A cave in Gull Rock (below).

minded. For me, the other wildlife highlight of the trip was the razorbills and guillemots seen on Gull Rock just off the coast from Nare Head.

What struck me most about the trip was the amount of sea that could be covered in this boat: within 30 minutes of watching the seals at Black Rock, we were sitting off Dodman Point, and that was with a break in the middle to look for wildlife activity. The boat trip is best described as exhilarating, and the fact that we didn't see a huge amount of wildlife made the commentary along the coastline even more important, so we popped into Portloe harbour and had a good look at St Anthony Lighthouse, along with a few tales told in Matt's inimitable and humorous down-under style.

Portloe seen from the boat (above).
St Anthony Lighthouse from the sea (below).

Would I go again? Well, I certainly enjoyed the two-hour trip, and would not be put off going again, though it would be the lure of potentially seeing dolphins that would attract me back, so I will be keeping a close eye on the Orca Sea Safaris' website to check on their latest sightings.

June 19th

Choughed to Bits

A pair of young choughs among the hottentot fig on the cliff slopes.

The fact that the chough was important enough to our Cornish forebears to have been included on the Cornish coat of arms, along with a fisherman and a miner, tells us something about the esteem in which this bird has always been held in the county. Cornwall is the only county in England to have breeding choughs, but even here they were unable to breed throughout the second half of the twentieth century.

The link between the miner and the chough was a stronger one than we might immediately think, and the decline in one certainly led to the decline of the other. While mining in the county was assured there were many pit ponies and donkeys in Cornwall, many of them grazing the coastal areas. This grazing produced the desired habitat for the chough, and as soon as the ponies were removed the chough's demise was signalled. Prior to the start of this century, the last choughs to breed successfully in Cornwall did so in 1947. What I find amazing is that the last surviving Cornish bird, born in 1947, is said to have lived until 1973, reaching a ripe old age of 26!

Now much more of the coast is grazed again. Conservationists have reversed the decline in the coastal fringe by introducing old breeds of cattle, sheep, ponies and even goats to recreate a more vibrant habitat for our wildlife, including the choughs. Since 2001, when three choughs arrived

A view of the most southerly point at the Lizard from Pen Olver.

at Lizard Point, we have seen a gradual increase in breeding activity, with pairs having bred in at least three locations; but it is still the Lizard pair that dominate the headlines and grab attention. In their first seven years of breeding, they have raised an amazing 28 young choughs, and their offspring continue to spread around the west of the county.

I visited on 19 June because I had heard that the young had just fledged. This is often the best time to see them, because the young birds are reluctant to fly far from the nesting site; and because they are still dependent on their parents for food, the adults have to keep coming back to feed them.

The choughs are easy to identify: they have a wonderfully glossy black plumage; quite obvious red bills and legs; quite broad wings with splayed 'finger' tips, and an enthusiastic 'chiow' call. To top it all, when the young have just fledged they can often be seen flying in their family group, calling to each other.

They were easy to find. When I first spotted them they were on the cliff slopes near the nest site among the hottentot fig. The adults were feeding the young, and the clamour of the youngsters for more food was loud and clear. The two adults would fly off towards Caerthillian Cove, and return five minutes later with more food; then they would spend time trying to teach the youngsters how to find their own. Thus far, the young had dug and probed quite aggressively, but not come up with very much of their own… but it is early days!

Both adults vigorously preening a young chough (above).
Six metres away, and I was chuffed (below)!

The young choughs are easily recognized, since their bills are not as red, nor are they yet as long as their parents'. They are also adorned with a ridiculously obvious set of rings on their legs. This ringing will help us to better understand their movements, but I always feel that it is a bit of an imposition, and aesthetically unsatisfying.

As the sun climbed higher in the sky, it generated enough heat for the birds to relax a little and enjoy the feeling of the sun on their backs.

An adult sunbathes (above).
One of the breeding pair of choughs (below).

Indeed, the choughs would spread their wings and absorb as much heat as possible. One of the most moving scenes I witnessed during the morning was of the mutual preening between adults and young; at one point, both adult choughs were preening the same youngster quite forcefully with their sharp bills. I can only assume that the open-beaked expression on the face of the young bird was one of ecstasy; it certainly showed no desire to move.

During the morning, I had many intimate moments with the birds, none more so than when one of the youngsters popped up at the edge of the cliff just beneath my feet. It is often the case that birds will come closer to you than they will allow you to get to them. I know this bird was only about six metres away from me, because I couldn't focus on it until I moved back a metre or so. I managed to get my closest-ever photograph of a chough, and you could say that I was well chuffed!

June 22nd

Damsels and Dragons

Steve Jones at Great Wheal Seton.

Since this is the end of National Dragonfly Week, it seemed an appropriate time to go looking for these wonderful creatures. Rather than going to a location that I had previously visited, or having a blind stab in the dark, I decided to enrol the help of Steve Jones. Steve lives close to me in the village of Godolphin, and he has various responsibilities associated with dragonflies in the county. He is the county recorder for dragonflies, so he collates records from active dragonfly enthusiasts and logs these on to Darter, the appropriately named database of the British Dragonfly Society. Using these records and his knowledge of dragonflies, he also provides guidance to environmental agencies involved in dragonfly conservation whenever this is requested.

Interestingly, Steve also sits on the Odonata Rarities Committee. 'Odonata' is the name given to the order of dragonflies; this is further split into two sub-orders, known as damselflies (*Zygoptera*) and dragonflies (*Anisoptera*). The use of the term 'dragonfly' as an order as well as a sub-order can lead to confusion, so dragonflies belonging to the sub-order *Anisoptera* are often referred to as 'true dragonflies'.

Clockwise from top left: A keeled skimmer newly emerged from its exuvia.
A small red damselfly: note the red legs and entirely red abdomen,
which help to separate this from the large red damselfly.
This scarce blue-tailed damselfly had probably emerged a few hours previ-
ously, and is clearly developing the orange colour of a female.
A scarce blue-tailed damselfly, which had emerged in the last half an hour.

From top: An immature female scarce blue-tailed damselfly.

An adult male scarce blue-tailed damselfly.

An adult male blue-tailed damselfly (for comparison).

The word *Zygoptera* is Greek, meaning 'paired wings'. This reflects the appearance of the damselfly's wings, which are folded parallel to its body (with the exception of the emerald damselfly, which holds its wings partly open). The term *Anisoptera* means 'different wings' – a name that came about because their wings are out-stretched, and in this position it is possible to see that the fore wings are different in shape from the hind wings. The other main difference between these two sub-orders is that damselflies are daintier than dragonflies; as a rule of thumb, if the body of a dragonfly is thinner than a matchstick, then it is a damselfly.

There are 39 species belonging to Odonata in Britain, of which 22 regularly breed in Cornwall, but occasionally we receive influxes of migrant dragonflies from overseas. When such records are received, they are checked by the rarities committee in exactly the same way as happens in birdwatching circles. Each record is assessed according to how thoroughly the identifying details have been recorded, and taking into account whether or not there is any further substantiating evidence, such as other observers or photographs.

Recent rarity records have included the scarlet darter (1995) and yellow-winged darter (1995 and 1996) and, exceptionally, a green darner which arrived from America assisted by Hurricane Earl in September 1998. Two other species – the red-veined darter and lesser emperor – which, until recently, were recorded only as migrants, now breed irregularly in the county.

Of the breeding species found in Cornwall, there are four which are used to define a 'Key Site'. These are scarce blue-tailed damselfly; small red damselfly; ruddy darter (now possibly extinct as a breeding species in the county), and white-legged damselfly. One other, the keeled skimmer, is often used to substantiate the site's status. These species are nationally scarce, and yet found in reasonable numbers in some parts of Cornwall, so it is important that we protect them, and this is why their breeding locations have become known as 'Key' sites. There are 63 such sites in the county, and when I asked Steve to choose a location for a day out, he chose one at which we could expect to see three of the five mentioned species. What he didn't do was to choose an attractive location for a picnic by a pond, so he warned me that it wouldn't be pretty; but he didn't tell me why he was taking his latex gloves!

A nearly mature male scarce blue-tailed damselfly.

Great Wheal Seton is situated in the Red River Valley – that is the Red River which flows through Tuckingmill and out to sea at Gwithian (just as there is more than one 'White River' in china clay country, there is also more than one 'Red River' in mining country). The name of the Red River came about because the pollutants, which it carried from the mines around Camborne, made it a deep reddy-brown colour. The heavy metals that were carried by the river would have had a negative impact on the natural history of the area at the time, and the fact that the soil has been laced with these compounds since then has prevented the substantial growth of vegetation.

It is an irony that these conditions have helped to create one of the most important sites for dragonflies in the county. The very fact that little vegetation can grow has allowed several unusual species to live here for many decades. Take, for example, the scarce blue-tailed damselfly. This is usually a species which lives in newly formed pools with bare edges, but here it can live happily in the longer term because the natural succession of plants is inhibited.

More specifically, the scarce blue-tailed damselfly likes shallow water in which to breed. Shallow water is good because it warms up well in the spring, allowing the larvae to develop quickly. The problem with shallow water is that it is also prone to freezing in the winter, which would kill the larvae; so success requires shallow water with a slow flow, which prevents it from freezing.

More or less as soon as we arrived, Steve found some larvae of this species, as well as several exuviae. An exuvia is the shed skin left behind by an emerging dragonfly, and, as Steve pointed out, seeing an exuvia or a larva is more important than seeing an adult dragonfly. Seeing either one of these two stages of the dragonfly's life cycle is conclusive evidence that the species has bred here, whereas seeing an adult dragonfly might be more exciting but cannot be used to determine successful breeding at the site.

Shortly afterwards, we found some newly emerged damselflies. The first had emerged with its wings stuck together, and despite Steve trying to separate them with a blade of grass, it was unable to fly. It is such a shame that, after spending a couple of years as an underwater larva, its ability to fly for the remaining days of its existence is ruined by a mishap during emergence. Yet the metamorphosis of an adult dragonfly from an underwater larva is one of the most dramatic and wonderful of any creature on the planet.

During emergence, scarce blue-tailed damselflies are pale green, but soon their colour changes significantly, with the females becoming at first a striking orange colour. Until fairly recently, it was thought that individuals of this colour were of a different species variation, but now it is appreciated that this is just a phase that all females go through for a short time. Once they reach adulthood, the females have a green thorax and black and green abdomen, while the males have a black- and blue-striped thorax and a black abdomen with blue in the tail.

This species can easily be confused with the much more common blue-tailed damselfly. Looking more closely at the males of these two species, it can be seen that the blue-tailed damselfly has just one complete blue segment in its tail, with an entirely black section beyond it. The scarce blue-tailed damselfly has one completely blue segment, but also a bit of blue in the segments on either side of it, leading to a much less distinct black end to its tail.

At the same location, we recorded eleven types of dragonfly, including the small red damselfly and keeled skimmer, both key species. After recording our sightings diligently, Steve left me to take some photos, and it was only then that the latex gloves emerged. The last time I saw a man pulling on latex gloves like this was in an episode of 'All Creatures Great and Small', and what followed wasn't pleasant, so I was quite relieved when I found out why he had brought them. Unfortunately, just like many other old mining sites, this spot is often abused by the younger generation in the area, and a whole host of rubbish can be found dumped here. Steve did his best to collect as much as he could, and we took a dustbin bag of wet rubbish home with us on the back seat of my car. Presumably, that also explains why Steve was happy for me to give him a lift!

July 1st
A DIY Guided Walk

It was in the June edition of the *BBC Wildlife Magazine* that I saw a review of a series of butterfly walks created by the National Trust on their own land. These walks have been published on the National Trust's website, so I decided to take a look at what was available for Cornwall. Just one had so far been uploaded, and though it didn't seem to be specifically aimed at butterflies, it did pick out a couple of special species that might be seen, as well as a wide range of flowers and other wildlife.

Kelsey Head seen over Holywell Bay.

The walk takes in West Pentire, Porth Joke, The Kelseys and Holywell Dunes. Embarrassed as I am to admit it, I had never walked through Holywell Dunes or on Kelsey Head, so I felt compelled to put that right.

The walk gets off to a good start at West Pentire, since it is here that the poppies and corn marigolds can be found flowering in the arable fields on the headland. It seems to me that these fields haven't been as impressive in the last few years, perhaps as a direct result of the change in the agricultural subsidy system which was supposed to benefit our natural history. One specification of the new system is that land should not be ploughed in the autumn or winter, because this can lead to soil erosion during winter storms. Unfortunately, poppies germinate best in autumn-ploughed fields, so the net effect is that there are fewer poppies here than there used to be. However, there is still a wonderful vista of corn marigolds each year, as well as a wide selection of other arable weeds.

Porth Joke is always a delightful place to spend time. Incidentally, Porth Joke – also known as Polly Joke – was once *poll an chauk*, meaning 'the chough's cove', but it is a long time since choughs bred here. My own memories of Porth Joke have been affected by a recent occasion on which I was almost arrested! I was happily minding my own business, photographing wildlife with a reasonable sized lens on my camera, when

Holywell Dunes.

I noticed a couple on the other side of the cove staring at me. I thought nothing of it, and carried on towards Kelsey Head, when I found myself confronted by two policemen wearing stab vests. After asking me a series of questions about my activities, it turned out that I had been reported as a possible terrorist. It is true that I had a bit of stubble on my chin and was wearing camouflage, but my lens was not an anti-tank gun or ground-to-air missile launcher, as had been suggested!

The policemen seemed happy enough with my story, as well as my photographs, and left me in peace. They probably received a questionable report and wouldn't normally have followed it up, but because it was a nice day and they were being given the chance to walk across the beach at Porth Joke in pursuit of a wildlife photographer, rather than the streets of Newquay in pursuit of real criminals... well, who can blame them? But later the same day, from the headland I saw army landing craft performing manoeuvres, and that explained why they had taken this particular report seriously.

Back to the walk. From Porth Joke, the guided walk rounds Kelsey Head. This is a great place for wildflowers, and it was still clear that there must have been a mass of thrift in flower here earlier in the year. Whether it would compete with White Island or not remains to be seen; in fact, I have already made a note in my diary to return in mid-May next year to find out.

After the Kelseys, the footpath enters the dunes of Holywell. Here it was difficult to miss one of the two target species of butterfly, the dark green fritillary. This is a very active species, but is thankfully quite large

Kelsey Head with corn marigolds of West Pentire in the foreground (above).
A pair of silver-studded blue butterflies (below).

and colourful. Typical of the fritillary family, it has an orange and brown chequered pattern on its back, but underneath it has a greenish suffusion, which is the reason for its name.

I had to wait for the return leg of the walk across the inland section of the Kelseys to find my first silver-studded blue butterflies. This tiny butterfly has a wing span of between two and three centimetres (about an inch), which means that when its wings are closed it is smaller than a five-pence piece, and can disappear almost completely out of view. To assist with this disappearing act, the silver-studded blue butterfly is much less colourful on its under wing than it is from above. The ground colour of the male's under wing is greyish-brown with a dusting of blue scales, while the female is dull-brown. Both male and female have a jumble of black and white spots on their under wings, as well as an organized band of black, orange, blue and white spots at the fringe of the wings. In fact, it is the shiny, silvery-blue element of this fringe of spots that led to the butterfly's name.

A male silver-studded blue resting on a pyramidal orchid (left), and the dark green fritillary (right), which is common in summer on the dunes of Holywell. It isn't uncommon to share the beach at Polly Joke with cattle (below)!

During periods of sunshine, these little butterflies take to the wing, revealing their upper wing colour, and this is when they are at their most striking. The male silver-studded blue has a wonderfully rich silvery-blue sheen, and his narrow black border and white fringe serve to frame his form beautifully. As is so often the case, the female is less colourful; in fact, it is difficult to accept that she is of the same species, being basically chocolate brown in colour with only occasionally a slight hint of blue at the base of the wings.

The directions provided by the National Trust are excellent, and the details of species to be seen are accurate, though this is where the idea of a DIY guided walk has its problems. Some of the species listed are extremely rare, and wouldn't be seen if I spent a month looking for them; some can be found only at very specific times of the year, which are not always stated; and some are difficult to identify, even if they can be found. Add to that the natural vagaries of wildlife-watching, and the outcome is that the user doesn't see everything listed. Mind you, it wouldn't do to see everything first time, because then we might not be tempted to return.

July 2nd

Huffin' and Puffin' around The Rumps

Yesterday I was at West Pentire, today Pentire; the two share the same name and yet they are not particularly close to each other. There is a simple explanation for this: the name 'Pentire' is derived from a Cornish word which simply means a headland, but this can obviously get confusing at times. Adjacent to Pentire Point is another headland, known as The Rumps. This name, so I am told, does not come from a Cornish word, but is simply a reference to the shape of this double-humped headland; I guess you probably have to see it from a certain angle to appreciate that one!

Every Wednesday from May to July, there is a guided walk around Pentire Point and The Rumps, but it has taken me three years to get my act together and get on one. The people leading the walks are knowledgeable enthusiasts; they modestly claim not to be experts, but certainly know enough to

The skies had cleared by the time we reached the other side of Pentire Point.

provide a stimulating commentary on flora, fauna and history. So much so that the walks have become incredibly popular, with sometimes as many as 40 people attending; fortunately today there were only five of us, including the leader, but that could have been due to the weather.

Crops grow on Pentire Point.

The weather certainly became a significant feature of the day. At times it was desperately wet; in fact, before we left Pentire Farm, where we parked, we had thunder, and during the walk it threw it down constantly for about 30 minutes, and this rain, unusually for Cornwall, was vertical in its descent, so not much chance of finding shelter on the barren Rumps. However, none of us were despondent about it, the reason being that between these extended showers, the light was absolutely sensational. The changing skies; moving light and shadows on the landscape; rumbling thunder over the sea; big waves breaking on the island offshore; fantastic visibility between the showers, and occasional big black clouds! Out on the desolate and prehistoric headland of The Rumps, it is impossible to feel anything but insignificant in this huge landscape, but this is what makes Cornwall so special.

The guided walk follows a fairly straightforward route. Starting at Pentire Farm, it rounds The Rumps and Pentire Point before returning up the small valley from Pentireglaze Haven. In total, it can only be between two and three miles. It would probably take about an hour and a half to walk it at a reasonable pace. The guided walk was scheduled to start at 10 a.m. and finish at about 3 p.m., and I couldn't believe that it would take that long; but it did, so this isn't a guided walk for impatient people. I had to smile wryly when, half-way through our walk, the lady who came asked our leader, 'How long have you been doing this walk?' I think we all knew what she meant, but, being me, I had to reply on his behalf, 'Only about three hours!' To be honest, I was quite impressed with myself for coming up with the retort so quickly, and fortunately everyone saw the funny side, and the fact that they did demonstrates the comfortable feeling generated between the people taking part on the walk. There was no stuffiness, no elitism, no competition and, though the weather was stormy, the ambience was calm and relaxed.

We did quite well to see a good range of birds, starting with several corn buntings around the farm and adjoining fields. The corn bunting is a very rare bird in the south-west of England, being found only along the north coast of Cornwall between Trevose Head and Pentire Point. To most people, I would imagine that the corn bunting is a drab-looking bird, but I enjoy the subtle differences between this bird and others that have some superficial similarities. Its most wonderful feature is its song, which is often likened to the jangling of keys. Fortunately, it is a bird that tends to perch on fence posts or even on chimney pots, as one did today, to produce its distinctive song.

Also common around the headland are numerous skylarks which, like the corn bunting, nest in and around the arable fields of the farm. Unlike the corn buntings, they usually sing from the air while hovering, but occasionally can be seen singing from walls and fence posts.

One of the main reasons for visiting the area at this time of

From top: A corn bunting in song is a regular sighting on this walk.
The skylark is commonly seen around Pentire Farm and headland.
The stonechat is another common bird around Pentire Point.

year is the chance to see puffins. This is the only place on mainland Cornwall from where it is possible to see these delightful seabirds. They don't breed on the mainland, but use the offshore island known as The Mouls. From the very tip of The Rumps it is easily possible to see puffins on the

Our group watches puffins (below) on The Mouls from The Rumps (above).

island, though our leader's telescope was useful to increase the magnification. Get your eye in, and with binoculars it is also possible to identify the puffins in flight. Compared with the razorbill and guillemot, which also breed here, the puffin is quite short and stumpy. We probably saw about a dozen puffins here, though only three or four were on the right side of the island to get a reasonable view of them.

Other highlights of the walk included a couple of peregrines and kestrels; a lot of Manx shearwaters, and a good range of wildflowers around the coast. The weather wasn't really helpful for seeing many insects, though we did find both five- and six-spot burnet moths, and several common species of butterfly. Historically, the area has much of interest, most notably the remains of an Iron Age cliff castle on The Rumps, the walls and ditch defences of which are still clearly visible. But I won't go into any more detail – I wouldn't want to spoil your enjoyment when you come and experience the walk for yourself, and I do thoroughly recommend it.

July 7th

Ratty Comes Home

The water vole was once a familiar creature on the waterways of Cornwall, but since the late 1990s, there hasn't been a single confirmed sighting of one in the county. Immortalized as 'Ratty' by Kenneth Grahame in 1908 in his story *The Wind in the Willows*, the water vole is looked upon as a harmless, lovable creature. Much of the inspiration for this tale was derived while Grahame was staying in Cornwall, at both Falmouth and Fowey; indeed, he wrote the first drafts of this book while staying at the Greenbank and Fowey Hotels.

I think I can anticipate how Kenneth Grahame would feel if he could read the statistics about water voles 100 years on. They are: in the last twenty years, the British population of water voles has crashed by a staggering 90 per cent, making it our fastest declining species; its range has been decimated and, most notably for

A water vole in its natural environment.

us, its Cornish population is extinct: in fact, Cornwall is probably the only English county where water voles are currently extinct.

So what has caused this catastrophe, and what are we going to be able to do about it? Before answering these questions, I am going to look a little more closely into the secret life of 'Ratty', the water vole.

The water vole, *Arvicola terrestris*, has sometimes been known as the water rat, a description that has come about through some superficial similarities between the two species, including their overall size and

Water voles have a blunt nose, rounded body and short tail.

colour; but the two species are only distantly related. The water vole is very different in character, habits and appearance, with a rounder face than the rat, smaller ears and a blunter nose; it is altogether a plumper-looking creature, and though it does have a long tail, this is fur-covered and often unobtrusive, due to its posture.

Water voles are active both day and night; they feed on plant materials, particularly grasses and other waterside vegetation, including the leaves of sedge and flag iris, buds, roots and fallen fruit. Often, they sit fairly upright and use their front feet to manipulate their food, a little like a squirrel might do. Water voles are good swimmers; when entering the water they tend to make a distinctive 'plop' sound (which is often the sign that gives them away to the alert observer), the purpose of which is to warn other water voles that there is danger. Once in the water, they will swim away to the safety of their network of holes in the bank.

Nationwide figures for the population of the water vole suggest that it has suffered one of the most catastrophic declines of any British mammal. There are two main reasons for this: one is the loss of suitable habitat, and the other is the spread of the mink.

Habitat decline can include anything from the loss of waterways, particularly canals, ponds and ditches, to the changing use and poor management of waterside banks. Where these are reinforced unnaturally, they become hostile to the needs of the water vole. Should some stretches of the waterway become unsuitable for voles, then their population becomes fragmented into smaller groups; this, in turn, makes the species more vulnerable to predation, and possibly to subsequent localized extinctions. The escape, and intentional release, of mink from fur farms has caused massive problems for water voles. Unlike the water vole's natural predators, including the grey heron, owls, pike and otter, the mink actively seeks them out, rather than opting for other prey. Cornwall is one of the mink's strongholds in England, but fortunately even their population has decreased significantly over the past few years. It is estimated that their numbers have decreased in south-west England by about 78 per cent, but they remain widespread.

The River Hayle near Relubbus.

Our isolated geographical position makes a natural recolonization of the county by water voles highly unlikely, and yet the national Biodiversity Action Plan (BAP) for water voles states that they should be restored to sites where they were known to exist about twenty years ago; so there are plans afoot to give them a helping hand by releasing some captive-bred animals in the county. CWT has been examining Cornwall for the best possible places to take action, and attention has focused on the River Hayle and the Red River (the one which flows out to sea at Marazion). It is known that water voles used to be found on the River Hayle and on Marazion Marsh, and since these two river catchments come close enough together for water voles to transfer naturally between them, this seems like the ideal spot.

If such a reintroduction of water voles is to be successful, we need to be sure that we won't simply be providing rich pickings for the mink, so a concerted effort to eradicate mink from this area would be required, probably for two years prior to any release of water voles. The Red River and River Hayle are well situated for such work, since this is the narrowest part of the county, and being in the tip of Cornwall it might be possible to eradicate mink from the district of Penwith, and only need to defend against them recolonizing from the east.

Face-to-face with a water vole (left).
Not big enough to be a water vole, this is a bank vole (right).

The reintroduction of water voles will be part of a much bigger project, which aims to enhance the wetland habitat in the catchment of these two rivers. This will obviously be important for the water voles, but will also improve the area for other wildlife. Land situated between the two catchments will be targeted for wildlife-friendly management to create a landscape-scale environmental project.

None of this will be possible without the support of the local communities. So, on 7 July, I was invited to attend a water-vole awareness day on the banks of the River Hayle, which had been organized for pupils of St Hilary Primary School. Kindly hosted by the River Valley Caravan Park near Relubbus, this day comprised of numerous activities, and 70 children from the school. The children were able to meet a real-life water vole, as well as learning more about the natural history of the river; water conservation; using the Cornish language to describe the characters in *Wind in the Willows*, and expressing themselves in poetry.

They clearly enjoyed their activities on the river bank. Let us hope that what they learned they will remember, because the future success of any projects we undertake will one day depend upon their understanding.

July 13th

Spraint Sniffing

Continuing the riparian theme, it's time to tackle otters. There is nothing quite like local expertise when it comes to finding our more elusive wildlife. Fortunately, CWT has many volunteers operating all over the county, and there are several local groups holding events and walks in their own areas. One such group, the Mid-Tamar Valley Branch, had arranged a walk along the River Inny from Bealsmill to its confluence with the River Tamar to look for signs of otters. Being private land, I knew I wouldn't get the chance to walk here on my own, so I took the opportunity to visit with them.

Otters are doing incredibly well in Cornwall, and all of our rivers show evidence of their activity, but because it is so difficult to see them in the flesh, recorders spend most of their time looking for their tracks and signs. Fortunately, otters are prolific in marking their territo-

A large stone in the River Inny.
Can you spot the spraint?

ries. Not only do they leave lots of droppings, they also leave them in fairly obvious places. We were only a few metres into our walk when we found our first example of an otter dropping, or spraint, as it is known.

Otter spraints are quite easy to identify. They are almost black and contain mostly fish scales, but it is their smell which is most characteristic. Get your nose close to an otter spraint, and fill your lungs with a sweet, fishy

Part of the Mid-Tamar Branch of the CWT walk through meadows beside the River Inny.

smell; I like to compare it with fish-flavoured candyfloss. These spraints are not always very big; in fact, many are quite small for such a big animal, but the fact is that the otter is leaving the spraint not just to relieve itself, but to leave a message as well. The message might have several meanings to other otters: it might simply be informing them that this is the territory of a male; or it might be used as a sign that there is a female in season, or that this is a good feeding area; we simply don't know. What we do know is that otters will leave spraints even if they have no faeces to pass; in such circumstances, they leave anal jelly, which has the same smell but lacks any dietary waste.

On our walk, we found spraints in the riverside grass; beside a run up from the river; among a pile of pine needles where otters seemed to have played, and on several stones protruding through the river's surface.

You will now be aware that we have had a lot of rain in the weeks leading up to this event, so the river was swollen. This meant that animal tracks had been erased from the river bank. The slight lowering in level over the last 24 hours had exposed only a fraction of the beaches that would otherwise have been present, so our opportunity to find otter tracks was severely diminished. In fact, the only prints we found were of poor quality, though good-quality otter prints are quite easy to identify. Otters have five toes on each foot, and each has its own pad, but they are asymmetrically placed, so that the outside pads are further back than the inside ones. The only other sign of otter activity was a damaged tree root where

A good example of an otter track (left). Note the five pads on each footprint, and the swish of its tail. Otters are now widespread in Cornwall, but seeing one (right) remains rare. An otter spraint (below), found under pine trees.

an otter had been scratching, a little like a cat does.

Having been on a walk with otter experts, I now feel much better placed to go out and search for signs of otters on other rivers. I can see that Sarah will be less than pleased when I insist on stopping every few metres to have a sniff of some likely-looking faeces, but personally I feel that it could become quite addictive.

July 18th

A Life on the Ocean Wave

In most years, the Isles of Scilly Steamship Company sends the *Scillonian III* out to sea for a day, past the Isles of Scilly and directly out into the Atlantic, with lots of people and plenty of barrels of festering fish guts on board. You may be wondering why, and I wouldn't blame you for questioning the sanity of anyone who would want to spend about 15 hours rolling around on a boat in the middle of the sea, particularly when the smell of rotting fish guts is released into the air.

The reason for this strange behaviour is birdwatching. Out there in the Atlantic there are species of bird to be seen that are rarely, if ever, seen from terra firma. One species in particular has attracted a great deal of interest on these trips – the Wilson's petrel, which is now seen regularly on the *Scillonian* pelagic; the area in which it occurs has been nicknamed the Wilson's Triangle.

The fish guts aren't taken along just for the ride. When the *Scillonian* reaches the Wilson's Triangle the chum, as it is known, is tipped overboard. The stench, which can turn the stomach of even a seasoned seagoing traveller, actually attracts petrels to come and feed. Petrels have a surprisingly good sense of smell, and are lured from miles around, along with many other seabirds, including shearwaters, gulls and skuas.

This trip appeals to dedicated, hardcore birders and twitchers. It's only a few years ago that I was one of those people; the smell of chum is still fresh in my nostrils, and the rolling feeling of a day spent on the *Scillonian* is still fresh in my mind; in fact, it took me about three days to learn how to walk in a straight line again! I like to think that the people who take part in this pelagic experience are eccentric rather than simply insane, but I must confess that after that trip I vowed never to do it again.

Therein lay a quandary, because this year I also vowed to take part in as many interesting wildlife events in Cornwall as I could. For once, fortune was on my side; the day of the pelagic was to be 10 August, and I already had plans for that day... I don't mean I was washing my hair! To compensate for this failing on my part, I decided to do the next best thing

Early morning, Penzance, from the Scillonian *(top).*
Paul Semmens looks carefully at seabirds following a trawler, while I try
unsuccessfully to keep my horizon level (above)!

– a day trip to the Isles of Scilly on a Friday. It has to be a Friday, because it is then that the RSPB has a member of staff on board to help show people what sea life is around. Also, for RSPB members there is a reduction in the fare, making this an extremely good value day out. Compared with a full day pelagic trip, this is much more mainstream, with only two bursts of three hours each at sea, and with a longish spell on the islands to boot. This is a much more sensible activity for most people, and fortunately the only chum likely to be seen on this venture is if somebody makes the mistake of eating a mackerel sandwich before venturing out to sea!

A common dolphin (above) rides the bow waves of the Scillonian, *in the calm water of September.*
   A guillemot (below) flies over sea. A sandwich tern with a sandeel (bottom).

My guide for the day was Paul Semmens. Paul is an extremely knowledgeable naturalist, and though he enjoys birds most it is quite clear that he has built up a vast knowledge of most aspects of our wildlife. He is also a friendly, easily approachable person, so is ideal for helping people to get the best out of their wildlife experience on board.

I was really looking forward to my day, but wondered whether I might have a slight anticlimactic feeling. Last year, in September, I took a week's break on the Scillies, and the trip out on the *Scillonian* was the most remarkable I had ever had. Without any assistance I saw Risso's and common dolphins; sunfish; porpoises; about 100 basking sharks, and plenty of seabirds. One of the reasons for my success was that the sea was absolutely flat calm; it was literally like glass, and I can't remember ever seeing it like that before or since. Those conditions are ideal for spotting cetaceans, because anything that breaks the surface is immediately obvious for miles around.

Today was not at all calm. The wind had got up and created quite a turbulence in the sea, and the crossing to the islands was going to be best described as choppy (maybe we would get some chum, after all!). I was a little heartened when Paul told me that, although the sea was a little too rough to be ideal for spotting cetaceans, a little bit of wind actually provided favourable conditions for seeing birds. It didn't take long to prove him right. I was extremely pleased with myself for finding our only Balearic shearwater of the trip before we had reached Porthcurno. Between there and Land's End we saw a plethora of Manx shearwaters and storm petrels, which gave us heart to work hard in our search for life at sea.

Peninnis Head on St Mary's, from the Scillonian *(above). The* Scillonian III *seen from Bar Point, St Mary's (below).*

I use the phrase 'working hard' advisedly. It is quite draining to spend three hours continuously searching over a fairly barren sea, but the rewards are there to be had, and it is much easier when there is someone to help. Before too long, Paul had spotted a sunfish which came close to the side of the *Scillonian*, and we saw guillemots and razorbills as well as common and sandwich terns as we approached the islands.

When we landed, at about noon, I was a little surprised when Paul suggested walking out to Peninnis Head so that we could do a bit of sea-watching! However, I could quite see the positive side to sitting on the headland in the sun having

Travelling on the Scillonian *is often rewarded with spectacular views, such as the one above of Tater Du lighthouse at sunset (taken on an autumn trip).*

our sandwiches, so I went along with the idea. He reckoned we might see porpoises from Peninnis, and sure enough there were four of them chasing fish around in as active a manner as I have ever seen porpoises.

A bit more walking; a cup of tea and slice of cake, and it was back to Hugh Town to board the *Scillonian* for the return leg at about 4 p.m. The sea had calmed a little, but there was still quite a swell which rolled us around more than on the way out; however, it was a smooth roll! There was a different group of people on the return, and a bit more interest in the birds, so with more eyes we did well to spot a marsh harrier (before we left the islands); a couple of great skuas; a puffin, and a small group of common dolphins, as well as the same things that we had seen on the way over.

All in all, I can thoroughly recommend this trip: a good range of wildlife; good company; good value, and a good few hours on Scilly. Now that isn't a bad way to spend a day!

July 22nd

In Memory of the Queen's Jubilee

The *Jubilee Queen* is a pleasure boat that sails from Padstow, built in 1977 (the Queen's jubilee year) by Brian Chapman, in a local boatyard in Wadebridge. Since then, for over 30 years, Brian has skippered this boat, taking people out around Pentire Point as far as The Mouls.

I intended to take a trip on the *Jubilee Queen* on the same day that I joined the guided walk around this headland on 2nd July, but the weather was so stormy that the boat wasn't putting to sea. Given less dramatic weather, there is the option of combining the two trips. For the energetic, it would be possible to park at Pentire Farm early in the morning; do a self-guided tour of the headlands; walk as far as Rock, and then catch the ferry to Padstow, from where the *Jubilee Queen* will take you to sea. For the less

The Jubilee Queen *sails from Padstow (top), and in the Camel Estuary (above).*

energetic, try a guided walk during the day, and then drive to Padstow for a boat trip in the late afternoon or evening.

For me, the only option was to return to Padstow when the weather improved. The boat trip travels out of the Camel Estuary to Newland Island, before heading around Pentire Point and The Rumps to circle The Mouls.

A row of shags (above) on Newland Island (below).
A view to The Rumps from the sea, showing the Sevensouls (bottom).

How interesting it is to get this different view of the headlands. From sea-level, their height seems to increase along with their dominance over the surrounding coastline. A commentary along the coast keeps up the interest, but for me it was the close-up views of the islands that made this trip attractive. Newland is devoid of vegetation because it is more exposed than The Mouls, and as a result it doesn't have any breeding puffins. Instead, nesting on its cliffs are gulls and shags. I was quite surprised by how close Brian could take the boat to the edge of the cliffs here, but I suppose the weather was good and the sea fairly calm.

A view of the Camel Estuary from near Padstow.

Before we reached The Mouls, we had already seen our first puffin – a single bird flying low over the water. It passed quite close to us, between the boat and the island, and it turned out to be the only one we saw. Evidently more puffins are seen here on overcast days than when it is sunny. I don't know why that should be, but it certainly matches my experience. We also saw razorbills and guillemots on the island, as well as many more shags on its summit.

Highlights of the previous few days on the boat had included peregrine falcon and bottlenose dolphins, while most summers there are regular sightings of sunfish and basking sharks. Strangely, though, this year has been a very poor one for basking sharks. This must be due to the availability of food, which for the basking shark is plankton. It might just be that the plankton is very much deeper in the sea because of the rough conditions, so we are not seeing the basking sharks at the surface.

August 20th

The Helford

The Helford River is hugely significant for wildlife conservation in the county, and yet it remains an enigma, even an anomaly, to many of us.

The enigma has been enhanced by its literary associations. The river comprises many smaller creeks with just one, Frenchman's Creek, being well known because of its association with Daphne du Maurier. Its geography adds to the mystique of this area, because much of it is very difficult to get to by road.

Its geography also provides us with the anomaly. The Helford 'River' is not easily recognized as a river at all. Despite the fact that its catchment consists of a significant portion of the Lizard peninsula and the area of land to the east of Helston, including Constantine and Mawnan Smith, the area that we know as the Helford 'River' is a complex of tidal creeks rather than fresh water.

It is interesting to reflect upon how these creeks were formed, because this might help to shed a little light on why we know it as a 'river' when it is essentially sea. Look at this river system from the air, or on a map, and you will see that the main river and subsidiary creeks take the form of a river valley rather than an open estuary. These valleys were formed at a time when sea levels were much lower than they are today, and they were formed by rivers rather than by the action of the sea. Over the last 10,000 years, since the end of the last Ice Age, sea levels have risen, and at Helford the valley has been inundated. Such flooded valleys are known as 'rias', and the Helford is one of the best examples of these in Britain.

Further evidence of the fact that these valleys have been flooded comes in the shape of the trees that now dip their branches into the sea water at high tides. In years gone by, there would have been further trees at lower levels which are now covered in mud, and we can still see trees succumbing to this rise in water, with occasional skeletons of once vibrant oaks stretching out across the muddy margins of the creek.

It is likely that the name of the Helford River came from the small village that sits beside it on its southern bank. Helford, or 'Hayle-ford', means literally 'the ford across an estuary', and since there is a ford across the creek at Helford, it is likely that the village was named first.

Sunlight breaks through the oak trees overhanging the creek (right).

A view from Nare Point, at the mouth of the Helford, looking back to Durgan.

This is consistent with many of the other creeks – most obviously Mawgan, Porthnavas and Gillan.

The Helford is special for wildlife because it is such an unusual habitat. It isn't really a river and it isn't really the sea, it is somewhere in between. The estuary is a nursery area for sea bass, along with many other fish (over 80 species recorded), molluscs and crustacea, such as oysters; it also has some unusual and very rare sea creatures, such as the fan mussel and Couch's Goby.

The Helford has a long history of oyster fishing. Prior to the nineteenth century, it was noted for having a great wealth of native oysters, but these were fished almost to extinction. Having had time to recover, this fishery is again an important part of the life of the Helford, contributing to its commercial success, though its management is now under much tighter control since it is situated in such an environmentally sensitive area. The native, flat, oysters are faring much better under current practices, and some Pacific oysters are being farmed to extend the seasonal availability of this shellfish.

Many sea creatures return to the Helford to breed, because of the safety afforded by the beds of eelgrass. Eelgrass is Britain's only flowering plant which grows completely submerged by sea water in muddy sand. Its value to the marine community in providing food, shelter and stability is extremely high, and though it has been through a period of decline, it now seems to be recovering. Look for it on very low tides, just offshore from Durgan beach.

Durgan is an attractive hamlet on the edge of the Helford River.

If you still don't believe how important the Helford is, then take a look at its designations: it is part of a marine Special Area of Conservation (SAC); its northern shore, near the mouth of the Helford around Rosemullion Head, was one of the first intertidal zones to be designated as a Site of Special Scientific Interest (SSSI), and now most of the intertidal area of the creek is a SSSI, as well as Merthen Wood, near Constantine; it is part of an Area of Outstanding Natural Beauty (AONB), and it has been designated as a marine conservation area since the formation of the Helford Voluntary Marine Conservation Area (HVMCA) in 1987.

It is this last point which helps the local community to become more involved with the Helford. Every year since 1987, a range of activities based around the river and its catchment area has been organized by a keen group of volunteers. Interpretive material has been produced to promote a better understanding of the environment, and so well organized has this group become that there is even a part-time paid secretary taking on the lion's share of this work.

Annual events with the group include a summer boat trip on a high tide up the Helford nearly as far as Gweek, and then out to the end of the estuary at Nare Point. This is a wonderful occasion, with lots of information about the river and some stunning views. In fact, it is far easier to see this river by boat than by car or on foot; much of it is difficult to access on narrow, twisting lanes.

Today, I attended one of their other activities – a rock-pooling ramble on Durgan beach. Durgan is a quaint hamlet on the northern edge of the river, close to Mawnan Smith. This stretch of the river is probably best known for its famous gardens, including Trebah and Glendurgan, both of which

The Helford River from Trebah Garden (above). A cushion star, a tiny, broad-clawed porcelain crab, and a pair of common blennies (below).
  Delving around in rock pools at Durgan (right).

are situated in attractive wooded valleys leading down to the river.

Despite yet another day of dismal weather, a good group of enthusiasts turned out to probe about in the rock pools. I wouldn't say we found anything particularly rare, but we had a lovely afternoon. My best finds included a pair of broad-clawed porcelain crabs; a couple of cushion stars, and lots of strawberry anemones; but it was the camaraderie of us all being involved in the same activity that was a highlight. It was good to have specialists there to help us identify anything we found, but it was even better to have a lot of children there. Getting kids involved in natural history is essential, and there is no better way than by rock-pooling. Just one thing, dads – let the kids have a go with the net… just sometimes!

August 22nd

Basking in the Sun

Carn Gloose headland.

The first decent weather forecast for weeks gave me the courage to get up early and join the Basking Shark survey team at Carn Gloose, near Cape Cornwall. Carn Gloose is a beautiful headland with terrific views, making it a great place from which to watch the sea. Just to the north is Cape Cornwall, while south of here is Sennen Cove. Out to sea are the islands known as The Brisons; slightly more distant is the Longships Lighthouse, and on a good day even the Scillies are visible. On the headland is Ballowall Barrow – a striking Bronze Age burial cairn. The remains of this monument were concealed by waste from the mining industry until the late nineteenth century, before being discovered by William Borlase. He unearthed the remains and built walls, which changed its appearance, but this remains a fascinating monument.

This is the second year in which there has been a concerted effort to survey basking sharks, as well as other oceangoing wildlife, from West Cornwall. In 2007, an amazing 656 basking sharks were spotted in 1,000 hours of surveying from Gwennap Head in the SeaWatch South West survey. This year, CWT has joined in to help organize a team of volunteers to watch throughout daylight hours for ten weeks. It is hoped that we will learn more about the sharks' behaviour, so that we can help protect them and their marine environment into the future.

Abby Crosby looks out to sea.

It is incredible that enough volunteers have been found to sit on this exposed headland to look out to sea for at best irregular sightings of these creatures. Particularly when you consider that on most mornings they have been here from 6.30 a.m., and that the weather over the last two months has been absolutely dreadful! It is for this reason that this summer will go down as the worst for sightings of basking sharks for many years.

Looking for basking sharks is particularly difficult in rough seas, not just because their fins don't break the surface very clearly, but also because their food – plankton – tends to be deep beneath the waves. The sharks are still out there in rough seas, but they swim at the depth of their food.

I arrived at about 7.30 a.m. to begin my bit of sea-watching, and a little later Abby Crosby, Marine Education Officer with CWT, arrived. She hadn't missed much. There weren't even many seabirds flying past as the sea was relatively calm, and the wind was from the north.

We sat and talked for about two hours, regularly scanning the sea for anything; but all we saw were gannets, fulmars and gulls. The best entertainment came from land, with a pair of buzzards hovering over the headland, and a pair of ravens honking away to each other as they displayed in the sun.

Other interested people stopped to talk, and the time passed quickly, but still no sightings of basking sharks, though the records showed that there had been two yesterday. I have no doubt that Abby was spurred on by that thought when I left her mid-morning.

Ballowall Barrow at Carn Gloose (above), and Cape Cornwall seen from Carn Gloose (below left).

The sight that remained elusive: a basking shark (below right).

Reflecting on it, I am not sure how much it mattered that we didn't see any sharks. The fact that we had sat and watched; chatted about the things that interested us both, and relaxed, was enough. And the next time I see a basking shark I will appreciate it even more than usual.

August 23rd

Hide-and-Seek

It is time for a day of serious bird photography.

One of my voluntary roles with CWT over the last ten years or so has been organizing events for their photographic group. Wildlife photography has become incredibly popular in recent years, and the advent of the digital medium has obviously had an impact, making this hobby more accessible.

My partner in crime is Adrian Langdon, an excellent wildlife photographer and committed conservationist. As well as undertaking voluntary work for the Wildlife Trust, he is a member of Cornwall Birds, and manages their premier reserve near Wadebridge, called Walmsley Sanctuary.

This is a wonderful freshwater wetland reserve, like no other in Cornwall. The range of wading birds that visit here in autumn and winter is phenomenal. Its success is due to careful

Walmsley Sanctuary from the tower hide.

long-term management, and that must be due at least in part to Adrian's intimate understanding of the place; it has been a bird reserve since 1939, and he has looked after it since 1997.

Management of Walmsley is mostly about getting the water levels right. The reserve is situated on the floodplain of the River Amble, but this river has been deepened and straightened so much, to prevent flooding, that it never floods any more. The water that now creates the reserve

The tower hide at Walmsley Sanctuary (above).
A peregrine falcon generated the greatest excitement of the day (below).

simply flows off surrounding land and is kept in place, or let through, by a sluice. Reeds and rushes are cut at least once a year to prevent them taking over, drying out the reserve, and cattle are grazed to provide a suitable habitat for flowers, insects and birds.

The terrific tower hide, opened in 1999, enables visitors to look over all of the pools and scrapes with ease, but it isn't much use for bird photography. It is surprising how close you need to be to a bird to get a decent photograph of it. So Adrian and I decided to have a photography session within the reserve. Last night, he set up a hide for us among some irises adjacent to a muddy area where wading birds had been seen frequently in the last few weeks. This morning, I crawled out of bed at 3.30 a.m., so that I could meet Adrian just after 5 a.m. at Walmsley. We needed to be in the hide before dawn, so that we didn't disturb any birds.

The approach to our hide, in darkness, was unfamiliar to me. We wandered across several fields, over stiles and through gates, before eventually reaching the far end of the reserve. Walking through the rougher vegetation of the reserve was difficult. We were fully laden with photographic equipment, as well as a tripod and seat for the session. The ground underfoot was boggy and gave way to varying depths, occasionally threatening the tops of our wellies,* but we wouldn't have known much about that until the inevitable damp, cold feeling in our socks. The air was still, and with nothing to see the various scents were all the more apparent. The pleasant, sweet smell was of water mint, crushed by our feet as we fought our way through; the other, less pleasant aroma, was of marsh gas escaping where our feet penetrated the ground.

Adrian outside the hide where we had spent the last six hours (top), and me (above), ready to depart with hide on front and camera gear on back. No wonder I nearly sank without trace!

We reached the hide at about 5.30 a.m., and were settled within a few minutes. We had a fairly large hide, but it was cramped by the time we had both set up our tripods and stools, and laid out camera bags for easy access to our equipment. This was home for the next five or six hours: a little too compact and bijou, but with a good location and cracking views over a muddy scrape!

I can appreciate that not everyone would want to spend a morning in this way, and that is fine: if they did, I might be out of a job! However, it is exciting to be able to sit in such a wonderful place, unnoticed by the birds and animals, and simply watch what goes on. Nowadays, we all seem to rush around doing 'things'. How often do we get the chance to sit, wait and observe?

The highlight of our morning, in terms of birdwatching, came courtesy of a peregrine falcon. It had already buzzed over once, scaring a small flock of dunlin half to death when it came back for a second go, but this time at a black-tailed godwit. Neither Adrian nor I were really aware of what was happening when a black-tailed godwit suddenly splashed

A pair of black-tailed godwits.

down into a pool: it didn't so much land as ditch unceremoniously into the water. A split second after came the screech of a peregrine hurtling in from the west, but it missed, and the godwit took to the air again. Surprisingly, the bird got away by gaining height before the falcon could turn to mount another attack.

I am a little embarrassed to say that none of this was captured with our cameras; the action was a little too far away and was over in an instant, and the constant attention of the peregrine was probably the reason why very few birds came down to the scrape in front of us for the morning; those that did had a very nervous look on their faces!

Other highlights of the morning included a kingfisher, water rail, and some photos of little egrets and black-tailed godwits; but at about 11.30 a.m. we decided to pack it in for the day.

* I hope you will enjoy sharing one of the biggest laughs I have had all year:

When writing this part of the book, I checked the text with a spell-check, and without looking carefully enough accepted one of its suggestions. Luckily for me, I then sent the text to Adrian for him to check it too. He spotted an embarrassing and anatomically inaccurate line:

'The ground underfoot was boggy and gave way to varying depths, occasionally threatening the tops of our willies...'

Obviously Americans don't have wellies!

September 6th

The Reptile Challenge

Mark Nicholson is one of the county's top experts on reptiles and amphibians, and is the leader of Cornwall's Reptile and Amphibian Group (CRAG) – a specialist group, which, like the photographic group, acts under the umbrella of CWT.

In spring, I challenged Mark to take me out for the day and show me as many different reptiles as he could. I was generous in that I allowed him to choose the time, date

Mark Nicholson turns over a corrugated tin sheet to see what lurks beneath.

and location, but I was also a little sceptical about his chances of finding a good variety at any one location, because reptiles are notoriously difficult to find on demand.

Mark chose September for this reptile hunt. He explained that it is always best to look for reptiles in spring and autumn, because during the summer the temperature is often so hot (please don't laugh) that reptiles need to bask for only a very short time before they are warm enough to go off hunting. This wasn't going to be a problem today!

The choice of location was to be even more critical, and Mark decided to take me to the dunes inside the MOD area at Penhale. This area is not open to the public, but organized groups can gain access with permission from the MOD, and Mark already had a trip planned here along with a dozen 11- to 14-year-olds from CWT's Out and About group.

This area of the dunes is the richest for flora and fauna, with rare species such as marsh helleborine and fragrant orchid flourishing here. Significant dune slacks offer water for spawning amphibians, and some-

Two heads and no tail? This pair of slow worms was admired by the Out and About group.

where damp for grass snakes to hunt. For the reptile-spotter, there is the added bonus of tin sheets strategically positioned close to good hunting habitat.

Reptiles favour tin sheets because they can bask underneath them, even when the weather is less than perfect. But which species of reptile were we likely to find today?

In Cornwall, there are five species of reptile. Only one of these, the sand lizard, is really very rare. In fact, the sand lizard is found at only one location (not Penhale), and this is kept secret because the species has been introduced there in the hope that it can start a successful breeding colony.

Of the four that we might see today, the commonest is the slow worm. The slow worm is a type of lizard which has lost its legs through evolution; it can be found across the county in a variety of habitats including gardens and grassland. To find one, it is usually necessary to look underneath fallen logs, or inside compost heaps. Slow worms are quite small – usually no bigger than 30 cm long, and about as wide as a little finger. Males are plain grey in colour, while females have dark flanks and dorsal line.

The closest relative of the slow worm in Cornwall is the common lizard. This is a species which has legs and is very fast off the mark, which is why the common lizard is so difficult to spot. It is a widespread species in the county, favouring spots that combine longer vegetation with more open areas for basking. Common lizards rarely bask under tin sheets, partly because they have legs which make moving about in cramped spaces quite difficult. The common lizard is slightly smaller than the slow worm, being up to about 15 cm long, and its tail can account for half of its entire length.

We have just two species of snake in Cornwall, and the commoner of the two is also the only poisonous one: this is the adder. Adders are most common in grassland, particularly dunes, and on heaths, and they love basking under tin sheets. The diamond pattern along their backs is distinctive, and this provides good camouflage in many settings. The adder grows up to about 50 cm long.

The young grass snakes were the most popular of our reptiles. The one on the right decided to play dead.

Finally, we have the grass snake – a species which is not common in Cornwall, but which lives in areas of damp grassland and is frequently found in water, swimming in pursuit of prey. The grass snake is our largest species of reptile, growing to well over a metre in length; it has a striking yellow collar on an olive-green body. This is the only native species of reptile which lays eggs; the others generate eggs, but keep them inside their bodies until they are ready to hatch.

We were able to check under ten tin sheets at Penhale, and the commonest species, by far, was the slow worm. This was probably due to it not being too hot; generally, slow worms don't like tin sheets when they are really hot. I knew about the slow worm's defensive mechanism, which allows it to shed its tail when attacked, but I had never experienced a slow worm defecating when handled; however, this seemed to be effective in repelling an 'attack' from a group of small children!

The next most common species of the day was the grass snake. All the grass snakes were young ones – probably up to about three years old – and, as with the slow worm, I was intrigued by the defensive strategies these snakes employed. The first was to exude a smelly secretion from pores in their skin; this smell can be likened to dog mess, and would certainly put me off eating one. The other strategy is one which I have read about but never seen before;

The adder was the one reptile that we might have seen but didn't.

The common lizard was our final find of the day.

fortunately, today one of the grass snakes obliged by playing dead. It coiled itself up; turned upside down; opened its mouth, and stopped moving while in Mark's hands – a fascinating piece of subterfuge.

We were on to the final sheet before we managed to add to our tally of two reptile species, and to our surprise the final species of the day was a common lizard, possibly the least likely of the reptiles to be found under a tin sheet. The day passed by without us seeing an adder, which I found surprising, but on a dull day in September we weren't sad, 'cos three out of four ain't bad.

October 5th

Hawking

The nearest I come to taking part in country sports is when I play football with the dog in our top field, but this year, in particular, I made a promise to myself that I would keep an open mind about activities involving natural history, and try things that I might at other times shy away from. So when I received an invitation to go hawking for the day, I decided to accept. But how would I feel about a 'sport' whose aim is essentially to kill wildlife?

I felt a little furtive meeting in a lay-by beside a road in West Penwith to follow a car to our hunting ground, but I think this was only because most people would have had trouble finding the location for our hunt. To be honest, I was quite surprised and pleased by the low proportion of four-wheel drives in our party, and only a couple of people were wearing tweed.

There were just six people with two hawks (a goshawk and a harris hawk), and about five ferrets. The day started very slowly. Low cloud hugged the moorland of West Penwith, and even plunged into the valley where we were hoping to find rabbits. In fact, I don't think we saw a rabbit for the first hour and a half.

Playing football with Fetlar (above) is not exactly a country sport! One man and his hawk (below).

A portrait of the juvenile goshawk (above).

The ferret eventually emerges from the holes in a hedge (below).

We moved down the valley towards the sea, and the cloud started to lift. Many of the old Cornish hedges here had rabbit holes scattered liberally along them, and at last we saw some rabbits out in the open. On sight of us, complete with hawks, they scuttled off for the cover of their holes, but that is no defence against ferrets.

Only one hawk could fly at a time, in case there might be a dispute between the birds. The falconer with one hawk would stand on high ground, maybe on the hedge, so that the hawk would have a good view of the surrounding land, while one of the ferret-keepers would put a ferret down a rabbit hole. The rest of us would align ourselves in such a way as to encourage any escaping rabbits out into the open. Then we would wait.

Most often the ferret would simply trot back out of the hole or an adjacent one and be put back into its warm box; but about two hours after we had started hunting, one rabbit did break for it across an open field; a hawk was released and gave chase. The chase was a brief one as the rabbit reached cover and the hawk darted off after some other rabbits on a distant bank, which had plenty of time to get away, leaving the goshawk to crash unceremoniously into the hedge.

We still hadn't caught a rabbit when a ferret decided to go walk about. This one ferret disappeared down a hole and wasn't seen for about 45 minutes. Modern-day electronic wizardry allowed us to follow its progress, because it

The harris hawk after an unsuccessful flight (top).
The harris hawk with a catch (above).

was fitted with a radio-tracking tag, so we knew where it was, about half a metre below us, but we could do little about it! Eventually, and thankfully, before we had to start digging, the ferret re-emerged and returned to its box.

I was beginning to wonder why people ever went hawking, when at last a rabbit broke cover and was out in the open long enough for our harris hawk to get its bearings. The hawk hit the rabbit with some force, and the pair tumbled over along the ground before the hawk came out on top. To my eye it looked like a clean kill, but the falconer was quickly on the scene to make certain. The hawk was given a treat, and the rabbit taken away to provide food for the bird over the next few days.

To watch a hawk hunting in this way was impressive. The hunt was over in seconds, so blink or turn around and you would miss it. There can be little doubt that the hawk enjoyed the experience, and I can clearly see that the hawkers love their hawks, and that this form of hunting provides both with stimulation and excitement.

Hawking is a much kinder and more strategic method of rabbit control than the introduction of an indiscriminate disease such as myxamotosis, but I don't think we can really argue that hawking will ever provide a satisfactory way of controlling the population of rabbits. In four hours we eventually caught five rabbits, between the two hawks and six people. The speed at which the hawks make their kill is essentially what makes hawking humane, while further highlighting the inhumanity of traditional fox hunting and hare coursing, which some people still refer to as 'sports'.

October 11th

Up the Creek Without a Paddle

I have been on a few boat trips this year, but none on board a boat powered by sail. Today I was lucky enough to have been invited out on a shrimper called *Sterren-vor* (star of the sea) by its owner, skipper and friend Howard Newlove.

Sterren-vor is kept on moorings at Mylor, so Howard offered me the opportunity to sail across the Carrick Roads and then up some of the creeks on a rising tide in the afternoon. A shrimper is a relatively small boat, and apart from going along for the ride I was also interested to put to test the theory that wildlife isn't afraid of the close approach of a sailing boat.

The forecast for the day suggested cloud with a reasonable breeze, but it actually turned out to be sunny and flat-calm. The sea was still enough to reflect the shape of the oyster dredgers as we set our sails to cross the Roads. The waves, such as they were, created a pleasant, relaxing sound as they lapped against the hull.

Skipper Howard Newlove keeps a steady hand on the tiller.

I was surprised by how well the sound of birdsong drifted down from the Roseland. A flock of skylarks flew overhead, and a continual flow of red admiral butterflies fluttered by in the breeze.

Oyster-fishing in the Carrick Roads (above).
Sterren-vor *(below) was the 518th shrimper to be made.*

About an hour after putting to sea, we still hadn't made it to St Just-in-Roseland, so a little assistance from our motor was necessary to complete the journey to our lunchtime moorings at the mouth of the St Just Pool. Resting at anchor, we listened to the mewing of two buzzards over Messack Point; one was mobbed by a crow as it soared higher and higher in an attempt to lose this irritating escort. In the creek, we watched little grebes diving busily for small fish as the tide began to rise.

Setting sail again, I was soon able to test my notion that I would be able to photograph birds from the boat. Sitting on a mooring buoy on our route there was a shag. Gradually, Howard guided his boat skilfully towards

Notice the flat forehead of the cormorant (left).
The shag (right) has a well-defined forehead.

the buoy, estimating the proximity that he dared approach as well as the angle of light which might enable me to catch the moment on camera. Sure enough, this was one bird that didn't mind us getting in close, but it did raise a question for Howard. How do you identify a shag from a cormorant?

In adult plumage, they are quite easy to identify. The cormorant has a white cheek, while the shag does not. In breeding plumage, cormorants also have a white patch on the thigh, and some even develop some white in the head plumage. Shags are all dark, but with an iridescent green sheen to their plumage; in breeding plumage they have a crest at the top of their heads. Cormorants are much larger than shags, and though size isn't always an easy guide to identification, they are also much bulkier birds, with a much heavier bill.

Many of the shags and cormorants we see are juveniles, because it takes them two years to develop adult plumage. During these two years, both cormorants and shags have a variable amount of white or pale brown plumage on their breasts and bellies, making them more difficult to identify. With a close view, it is still easy to identify a shag, because of the shape of its head: it has a raised forehead, while the forehead of a cormorant is flat and almost level with the top of its bill. One final tip for distinguishing these two species is to watch the way they dive for fish. The shag makes a noticeable jump up before diving below the water surface, while the cormorant simply slips into the water with less effort.

Lunch over, we headed up the Fal as far as Smuggler's Cottage; Cowlands Creek as far as Coombe, and Restronguet Creek as far as Point. This is by far the best way to explore these creeks. Getting around on land around the steep-sided wooded valleys is often difficult, while from a boat the feeling is relaxed, and the views atmospheric and beautiful.

A view of Coombe from Cowlands Creek (above).
A modern yacht and a traditional shrimper (below).

Cruising along the creek near the King Harry Ferry we found a cormorant and a shag sitting on adjacent buoys, which enabled me to take further photos, and Howard could put his new-found identification skills to the test. Also here we saw little egret, grey heron and kingfisher around the water's edge. Even with a shallow draught, Howard wasn't keen on taking the *Sterren-vor* too close to the edge, so we mused about the possibility of taking out a couple of canoes to explore the creek edge.

It was in Restronguet Creek that we saw most bird life, with a rather late sandwich tern perched on a buoy (late because most would by now be heading south); a rather early pair of red-breasted mergansers (early because these are usually present in winter on the Carrick Roads), and excitement in the form of an adult Mediterranean gull which gave only tantalizing views as it soared up and away from our boat into the clear blue sky. What a beautiful day it had been.

October 13th

A Walk in the Woods

Today I went out for a walk with some Friends – not the usual sort of friends that one might go out with regularly, but a group named The Friends of Kilminorth Wood. They don't just organize walks in Kilminorth Wood, but also in the surrounding area, and today we visited Trenant Wood.

If you stand in Millpool car-park, in West Looe, and look across the river, you will be looking at Trenant Wood. Pull on a pair of waders, or bring a

A view over Trenant Woods towards West Looe.

canoe, and you could be in this woodland in a matter of minutes. Funnily enough, not many people do either of those things, and the alternative is to drive several miles along narrow roads to get to the only other access point, which, unsurprisingly, is little visited by people. I suspect that another reason why very few people come to this wood is that there is no car-parking marked on the Ordnance Survey map, and the only access 'road' is really just a track, which would discourage any speculative searching.

I wouldn't ever have come here if it were not for my Friends organizing a guided walk, and being a well-organized group they had even arranged for Malcolm Allen, Area Manager for the Woodland Trust, to lead us. Parts of Trenant Wood have been owned by the Woodland Trust since 1991, and with the addition of two further areas of land in 2002 and 2006, this is now their largest holding in Cornwall.

The wood sits on a steep-sided hillside in the bend formed where the East and West Looe rivers meet. This is essentially a spur jutting out

Looking up the East Looe River (above).
  My Friends pause for a break and a chat (below).

into the valley, with open high ground on top and woodland on the steep slopes down to the river. Our route took us along the western side of this spur, looking over the West Looe River and Kilminorth Wood; then along the eastern side, overlooking the East Looe River, before crossing over the high ground back to the car-park. None of these footpaths are shown as rights of way on an Ordnance Survey map, but modern maps do show it as an area of 'Access Land'. The Woodland Trust is happy for all of us to make use of these paths, and has provided a car-park for us to use.

Some of the many trees planted by the local community at Trenant.

A short walk from the car-park, along an access track, we came to the first part of the valley which is owned by the Woodland Trust. This was purchased in 1992, and consists of open terrain looking down to the valley of the West Looe River and across to Kilminorth Wood. It was this point on the walk that left me with my most lasting impression of the day.

Despite being only a few metres across a muddy river from Kilminorth Wood, in many ways Trenant Wood is very different from it. Over the valley at Kilminorth, the wood is dense and continuous; walking within it is beautiful, but glimpses across the valley are few and far between. Here at Trenant, there are large sweeping vistas across to Kilminorth and beyond to West Looe, and despite the ugly tarmac of Millpool car-park, this is a memorable view. At Trenant, we climb higher than in Kilminorth, and have open ground to enjoy tremendous views, and this was a theme that continued throughout the walk, with areas of grassland breaking up the trees to provide views in every direction.

Along this first section of the walk, the policy of the Woodland Trust is to allow natural regeneration of the trees by self-seeding. This might take time, but evidence of its success can already be seen. The trees that have established themselves are staked and marked, so that if the surrounding vegetation is cut these trees can be left alone. In the long term, this policy should create a more natural woodland.

Following the path gently down towards the noise of bottle banks being emptied in Millpool, we soon entered an area of Ancient Woodland. Ancient Woodland is defined as being an area which has had trees growing on it continually for at least 300 years. That isn't to say that the trees are all 300 years old. To identify Ancient Woodland, we tend to look for the presence of particular species of plant such as bluebells, wild garlic and dog's mercury, all of which grow only in woodland, spread extremely slowly, and wouldn't be present if trees had not been growing there continually for a very long time.

A tree damaged by a squirrel.

These trees, like many others in Cornwall, have not always been left to grow naturally. Up until about 80 years ago, they would have been coppiced regularly, creating timber for boat-building and charcoal for smelting. The Woodland Trust, aware that coppicing here would be unsustainable, has decided to allow these trees to attain their full height.

Having descended almost as far as the banks of the West Looe River, opposite Millpool, we then headed east and north along the side of the East Looe River into a section of the wood which has been owned by the Woodland Trust since 1991. Instead of being Ancient Woodland, this area was grazed until it was purchased by the Woodland Trust. The subsequent management by the Trust reflects a time when it operated a slightly different policy, so here many trees were planted in the 1990s, and a wide variety of natives were used.

Since the mid-1990s, this woodland has started to develop into a rather attractive feature, with the different hues associated with the various species of tree. The policy of leaving woodland rides is the same, and this continues to allow views of the surrounding landscape, as well as allowing people in the surrounding landscape to enjoy views of a mosaic-style habitat, rather than continuous woodland. However, the drawback of planting thousands of trees at any one time is that they become a magnet for many browsing animals.

It was here that Malcolm showed us evidence of damage to trees caused by wildlife. In a small area we found trees whose bark had been stripped by three very different mammals. The first was an oak tree, badly damaged a few feet off the ground by a grey squirrel, but continuing to grow; the second was a much younger sapling, whose bark had been less severely damaged by a roe deer rubbing off the velvet from its newly formed antlers; the third was a tree which had developed a wider trunk, which had been completely stripped of bark up to a height of about 25 cm by a rabbit. There is no real need to worry about this sort of damage; since the trees are planted quite tightly together, some are bound to be out-competed, and this is a form of natural selection.

The roe deer have moved into these woods in abundance. They enjoy eating fresh foliage, and having lots of newly planted trees is like us visiting a sweet shop. Even in the middle of the day, with a large group of us chatting all the time, we still managed to see a roe deer doe, but she didn't hang around once she had spotted us. Come here early in the day, and

You will need to be observant to see a roe deer fawn, but they are at Trenant.

walk quietly through the woods, and Malcolm reckons it is easily possible to see a dozen or so roe deer.

The land on top of the spur between the two rivers has belonged to the Woodland Trust since 2006. Until then, this land was used to grow crops, and it is still possible to see some of the arable weeds, such as field madder and field pansy, which would have grown among them. Now these arable weeds grow among thousands of newly planted trees still protected by their plastic guards. Some of these trees were planted by Friends of Kilminorth Wood, when they spent a day here in the snow in February.

This landscape will change radically over the next few years, assuming that the roe deer allow some of the trees to grow! Strategically placed gaps have been made in the trees to allow visitors to continue to enjoy the breathtaking views, but here two further gaps have also been left for a completely different reason. An aerial photograph taken during very dry weather revealed two rather strange patterns near the summit of the hill. Although there is no evidence from ground-level, there seem to be two circular banks, possibly of stone, just underground. We can't be sure what the purpose of these might have been, but to prevent them being destroyed by tree roots, these two spots have been left in grass for now. One day, we might wish to dig this site to see if we can find out more about how this location was used by our ancestors. One thing is for sure: high on this hill, above the steep-sided valleys of the East and West Looe Rivers, this would have been a great place for a defensive fortification.

Our walk was soon completed, but I left feeling very grateful to 'my' Friends of Kilminorth Wood for introducing me to a beautiful place which I would never otherwise have visited, and to the Woodland Trust for looking after it on our behalf.

October 15th

Smoke Gets in my Eyes

The view over St Ives Bay from near Knill's Monument.

Many years ago, I used to spend a lot of my free time doing practical conservation work on nature reserves. As my life changed, so did my priorities, and this kind of volunteering became a thing of the past.

Today, I brought the past back into the present by helping out with a conservation project at Steeple Woods near St Ives. The purpose of the exercise at Steeple Woods is to help clear rhododendrons from this Local Nature Reserve. Rhododendrons are not native to Cornwall, and *Rhododendron ponticum* swamps everything in its path, creating a dense, dark cover of evergreen growth, so preventing any of our indigenous species from growing, and therefore affecting our whole ecosystem.

Another problem for which rhododendrons are responsible is the spread of a fungal disease known as 'sudden oak death' (SOD). Rhododendrons carry this disease, and spread it to our native trees, so removing them from wild areas has taken on an even greater urgency across the county.

Steeple Woods covers an area of about 40 acres (16 hectares). Part of it is mature woodland, but a significant part was smothered by the

Beech trees grow in the mature woodland of the reserve (above).
Knill's Monument by night (below).

spread of rhododendron, so the task of removing it is huge. A working group of volunteers – the Steeple Woodland Project Group – has met here every week since 1999, and their work looks set to continue for a good few years to come, but it is possible to see the results of their labours by visiting Knill's Monument, where native heathland is now growing where rhododendrons once flourished.

The heathland on top of the hill has started to regenerate quite quickly. The rhododendrons that still persist have grown from seed left in the soil, and these will be dealt with as and when they appear. The plan for the rest of the site includes the planting of native trees, just as soon as the rhododendrons have been removed.

Smoke from the fire seems to follow us around!

The working party today was organized by the British Trust for Conservation Volunteers (BTCV). The BTCV organizes several practical working parties every week, visiting a wide range of locations across the county from their base in Tuckingmill, near Camborne. They have a minibus which picks up volunteers from that area and takes them to the chosen location.

Volunteers come from a very broad cross-section of society. There are retired people giving some of their free time to help a good cause; youngsters who find themselves between education and employment; adults who are out of work; people, like me, who find some reward from spending the odd day doing hard physical work; people on working holidays, and people looking for training in the use of practical countryside skills, such as hedge-laying and brush cutting.

People volunteer for a variety of reasons, but they won't come back if they don't enjoy it. Today we were dealing with rhododendrons that had already been cut down. Our task was to burn them; so we lit three bonfires on the site; dragged the large branches to the fire, and threw them on top. We worked in teams of three or four, stopping only for tea and lunch breaks.

This might not sound like particularly enjoyable work, but there is satisfaction to be gained through working hard and being physically tired. Our own lives may not allow us to work as part of a team, so the camaraderie of this kind of work can also be a significant part of the reward. For me, escaping from my computer for a day and simply carrying logs around, gave me time to reflect and think about issues that didn't relate to my own everyday hassles.

The only stress we felt today was in trying to keep our bonfires going. The leaves and twigs would burn quickly, but the thicker logs took a long time to catch fire. If the heart of our bonfire burned out, then we would struggle to refuel it. The smell of smoke was everywhere, and when I got home my clothes were full of it. Occasionally, my eyes would sting when the wind changed direction and blew the smoke straight towards me. Fortunately, I quite like the smell of wood smoke, and there is nothing like a distinctive smell for bringing back memories: I was immediately taken back twenty years, to a time when this was a regular occurrence for me.

Volunteers throw the cut rhododendron on to the bonfire.

Time will tell whether lighting bonfires will rekindle my own interest in practical conservation work, but I would urge anyone to give it a try. Having done some good for the environment today, I know we all went home with a clear conscience and slept well.

October 25th

Fungus Foray

Pauline Penna shows a small group how to identify an ink cap.

Autumn wouldn't be the same without at least one venture into the woodlands to see what fungi are growing, but unless you are an expert it is difficult to fully appreciate the variety of fungi that can be found in this environment. Today, I visited Tehidy Country Park for a walk organized by CC's Countryside Service, and led by fungus enthusiast Pauline Penna of the Cornwall Fungus Recording Group.

I was convinced we would have a productive day as it had been so wet and relatively mild – ideal growing conditions for mushrooms and toadstools. So you can imagine my surprise when I was told there weren't many fungi about, the reason being that the summer had been so wet that most fungi had peaked much earlier than usual!

Fungi, of which we have over 12,000 different varieties in the UK, are present through-out the year, but for much of this time they are hidden from our view, existing only as a root system, known as a mycelium. When conditions are ideal for them, they grow fruiting bodies which are intended to spread spores, allowing the fungus to spread to new areas. About a half of all fungi have capped fruiting bodies, and it is these which we know of as mushrooms or toadstools.

Now let's take a closer look!

There isn't a hard and fast rule that separates the use of the words 'mushroom' and 'toadstool', though in general the term 'mushroom' tends to be applied to a fungus cap that can be eaten; so a toadstool is either poisonous, or at least unpleasant to eat (the use of the word 'toad' is generally reserved for an 'unpleasant' characteristic).

Fungi are essential to life on earth, since without them nature would be unable to rid itself of waste vegetative matter. Just looking at the woodland setting, fungi are responsible for breaking down all of the leaf litter, fallen branches and tree stumps. What I wasn't aware of, though, is that fungi are also essential to the growth of a huge number of plants. It is estimated that around 80 per cent of all vascular plants grow to their potential only if supported by a fungus. Such fungi can be found growing around the roots of these plants, and break down compostable matter into a form that can be utilized by the plant; in return, the fungus can tap into the plant for nutrients. Fungi are also eaten by quite a wide range of wildlife. Many of the caps had been partly eaten by slugs and snails, but we also saw a grey squirrel carrying away a toadstool to be eaten, which is quite unusual for the well-fed squirrels at Tehidy!

It was interesting to see such a wide range and large number of people attending the fungus foray. I didn't think that fungi would have such a broad appeal, but with 30 people aged between about five and 75 (though I didn't ask!), I was proved wrong. Maybe part of the appeal is due to people eating fungi, so possibly they were hoping to take home some-

Dead man's finger (left) was the most macabre fungus of the day.

The tawny funnel caps, forming a huge ring (right), were probably the most attractive fungi we found.

A pair of clouded agaric toadstools (below).

Do you ever get the feeling you're being watched? Grey squirrels are omnipresent at Tehidy.

thing unusual for lunch. Indeed, one or two did have professional-looking baskets, into which they obviously hoped to put some mushrooms, but opinion was divided as to whether it is acceptable to collect fungi.

Picking a mushroom will not damage the whole fungus, because the cap is simply its fruiting body, so taking a mushroom could be likened to picking an apple off a tree. However, if we all went out collecting fungi indiscriminately, we would prevent a lot of fungal spores from spreading to create new fungi. This is why fungus collectors use baskets and not bags: the spores from collected specimens can continue to fall through the basket's weave as they walk through the woods. My own opinion is that we should leave nature to take its course; I rarely eat fungi, except where I can take one and leave plenty more *in situ*.

The other risk when picking fungi to eat is that many species are poisonous. Pauline told us about one fungus enthusiast who had died quite recently after eating a fungus that he had misidentified. One interesting story about the edibility of fungi, which Pauline told us, relates to the common ink cap, *Coprinus atramentarius*, which is edible but must not be consumed with alcohol. The combination causes palpitations and nausea, so this species has been used in drug therapy for alcoholics.

December 14th

Cake at Coverack

The cake representing the layers in the earth from the mantle to the crust, even with a representation of Coverack Beach on top!

I have been interested in geology ever since I developed a passion for fossil-hunting when I was a child, but after completing an 'A' level qualification in the subject my interest waned as I followed a career in mathematics, which I thought might be a safer bet. More recently, my enthusiasm for the study of the formation of the physical environment and the rocks that underpin our surroundings has been rekindled by Cornwall's wonderful geological history. There are few more interesting places in Britain for geology than the Lizard peninsula, so when I was invited for a slice of cake at Coverack, by local geologist Peter Ealey, who was leading a group there, how could I resist?

Little did I know that the cake was going to be part of the learning experience! This fantastic example of patisserie art had been crafted to interpret the layers of the earth's structure, and where the rocks that could be found on the beach at Coverack had originated. A cross-section through the centre of the earth would reveal at its centre a core made of a dense solid material, surrounded by liquid; around this there is a mantle, which is plastic, and finally a solid crust, on which we all exist. The crust comprises of 'ocean crust' and

A heap of stones on Coverack Beach, but what are they?

'continental crust', according to where it formed. Between the mantle and the crust is a discontinuity, named after a Croatian seismologist called Mohorovičić; fortunately, it is known as the 'Moho'. The importance of Coverack in this story is that it is one of only a very few places on earth where it is possible to see rocks that have their origins in the mantle, at the Moho and in the oceanic crust, which is normally inaccessible on land.

It was about 375 million years ago that the Coverack story began. At that time, part of the earth's mantle, normally some 10 km below the earth's oceanic surface, became molten and forced its way to the surface; this molten rock was to become the rock which we now call serpentine. This intrusion occurred in the Southern hemisphere, but through plate tectonics this part of the earth's crust was moved gradually northwards, and about 300 million years ago it collided with the land mass that was to become northern Europe, and welded on to the southern tip of what we now know as Cornwall.

Meanwhile, further intrusions of liquid rock occurred. Weaknesses and cracks in the serpentine allowed magma from around the Moho to squeeze through and form a rock known as 'troctolite', distinguished from serpentine by its white feldspar crystals. Its spotted appearance has led to this rock being known as troutstone, because it resembles a trout's skin.

The next set of igneous intrusions came from the lower crust. The resulting rock, which has been called a 'gabbro', consists largely of white

The so-called Giant's Fist has been created by wave power and the abrasive effect of sand.

crystals, making this one quite easy to identify at Coverack. When in its fluid state, it forced its way through the serpentine, truncating the veins of troctolite, and so allowing us to conclude that its emergence came later. Finally, there are veins, or dykes, of basalt, which cut through and across all other rocks and intrusions on the beach. Basalt had its origins in the earth's crust, slightly higher than the gabbro. It can be recognized because it is a very fine-grained, dark rock.

Our day at Coverack today started with trying to identify these four different rocks among the pebbles we found on the beach. We sorted these into basalt, gabbro, troctolite, serpentine and 'rogues'. The rogues consisted of bits of brick, granite (which might have been used in creating a sea defence in the past), flint (which is found on the seabed a long way offshore) and quartz. Once we had mastered the appearance of the rock types, we set about looking for the solid rock outcrops, trying to interpret what we saw. To the north of Coverack, the rock is all gabbro (from the crust), while at the south end of the beach it is all serpentine (from the earth's mantle). Between the two is where it gets interesting, with some troctolite (from around the Moho) and many veins, or dykes, of gabbro and basalt.

It was fascinating to be with an expert, and to be able to interpret the many different intersections of rocks and veins. Not only were we able to decide upon which intrusions came first, but we could see where crystals in the different magmas had crystallized in different ways. The white crystals in the gabbro, for example, elongated towards its margins, where it had been dragged against the surrounding rocks; this type of gabbro is known as flaser gabbro. We also found some interesting weathering patterns on the serpentine rock, and could see where the white veins of 'secondary serpentine' had been secreted through cracks in its parent rock, forming an irregular mosaic pattern.

At the end, Peter confessed that he hadn't had to work so hard for a long time. That was probably a result of us asking so many daft questions, but we found a huge amount of interest on this unassuming beach, and would have struggled to interpret the signs without him. We also struggled with the cake – one cross section through the earth's crust and mantle was enough for anyone, so I suspect Peter is still battling his way through the rest of it now!

We arranged the pebbles according to different types under Peter's tutelage. Those on the left are serpentine, the commonest rock on the beach. The ones on the right are the rogues – a wonderfully descriptive term for pebbles that don't originate here.

From the top: Serpentine rock with a vein of gabbro passing through it indicates that the serpentine was in situ *by the time the gabbro intruded.*

Weathered serpentine, showing veins of lizardite, or secondary serpentine.

A dyke of gabbro, showing where larger white crystals have formed at its margin, is known as a 'flaser gabbro'.

This is a complex picture, showing the intersection of three rocks (left). To help interpret the scene, serpentine is shown in red; gabbro in blue, and basalt in green (right). We can deduce that the serpentine formed first; this was then intruded by a dyke of molten gabbro, and finally the basalt cut through both of them. We know the basalt came last because it truncates the gabbro dyke, while the basalt remains in a straight line across the photo.

December 24th

Snowy for Christmas

When I set out to write this book during the year I was sure that I would be including a twitch at some point during the autumn. Actually, the autumn was great for rare birds, with several significant finds in west Cornwall and on Scilly, but when it came to the crunch I couldn't bring myself to join the hoards of twitchers and queue to see a rare bird found by someone else.

Yesterday's news changed all that. Reports came in of a snowy owl in West Penwith. Probably the bird that had spent part of the winter in a field on St Martin's had now ventured over to the moors near Zennor. It wasn't me but my wife, Sarah, who insisted that we go and see it, so how could I resist?

The instructions for getting to the bird were quite clear on the website: where to park; which footpath to take; how far to walk; when to turn left, and which way to face to see the owl. It's probably that sort of information that makes me feel less like a birdwatcher and more like a train spotter, but Sarah was really keen to see a snowy owl in the wild.

We drove along the windy road from St Ives wondering how many people would have come to see the snowy owl on Christmas Eve. We found about twenty cars parked along the roadside, and I must admit I had been expecting more. We set off along the path, where a steady stream of people were walking back the other way. 'Is the bird showing well?' I asked, 'Oh yes,' came the reply, 'just follow the path round to the left and keep going.'

The instructions had suggested that the route was about 800 metres. It took a full half an hour at full speed to get there, even though we were trudging along a well-worn muddy path that must equate to at least a mile, probably a mile and a half. I had been a little concerned that we had taken our dog along for the twitch, but I needn't have been. The snowy owl had attracted lots of different people to come to see it. There were the usual green-clad, telescope-toting twitching fraternity, but there were also plenty of inexperienced-looking people too. One lady was wearing a

The snowy owl twitch attracted a wider range of people than is usual for a rare bird.

white coat, and another was attired in a bright red one, so this was not a normal twitch.

On arriving at the spot where there were a few people looking up to the moorland on the other side of a small valley, we paused and had a quick look around. I was reluctant to ask someone to show me the exact location of a big white bird with a wingspan of one-and-a-half metres, so I scanned the area with my binoculars. I first spotted a rock that looked like it had a snowy owl on top of it, but soon realized that this was just a red herring. Eventually, I located the owl, but even with binoculars it was very small. This was a young male snowy owl, so he had lots of dark barring on his back, which made him look very much like one of the scattered fragments of granite on the moorland. He had his back to us, and occasionally turned his head to look in our general direction.

Fortunately, one helpful birdwatcher offered us the chance to look through his telescope; I hadn't brought mine as I had carried my camera gear with me instead. It was with great embarrassment that I took my camera out and set it up to take a photo, because I knew that I wouldn't get anything particularly worthwhile. Still, I wanted to record the moment for posterity, and this book.

Can you spot the snowy owl (above), or is it a rock?
 A good telephoto lens brought out the detail nicely (below)!
(Okay, I admit it... it's a captive snowy owl.)

I was amused when one chap asked if he could look at the images on my camera. He looked very carefully at my camera, and the direction in which my lens was pointing, before confessing to me that he had been looking in the wrong direction for the last half hour, and had actually been watching a rock! Stranger still, he had been directed to look at this rock by another chap who had a telescope. I wonder how many people had spent their time watching the 'snowy owl-shaped rock' with his assistance?

We all left happy. Sarah seemed content enough with her rather distant view of a snowy owl; I had a new 'tick' for my British life list; the dog hadn't scared anything away; and I seem inadvertently to have saved a man from watching a rock for the entire day!

December 26th

The Pinnacle of a Cornish Year

Before today, Sarah had tried several times to make it to the summit of Brown Willy on Bodmin Moor, Cornwall's highest peak. Her attempts had been foiled by a rare mix of bad fortune, including the changeable weather and a sprained ankle. Unlike Sarah, I had never actually set out to walk up Brown Willy, though I had made the short ascent of nearby Rough Tor on several occasions.

A view of Brown Willy from Rough Tor, taken on a calmer morning in the autumn.

Throughout the autumn and early winter, we have been promising ourselves that at the next opportunity on a fine day we would make the pilgrimage to Brown Willy together. It is a little surprising that it took until the end of December to find such a day, but I suppose Boxing Day is as good a day as any.

We arrived at the car-park early, in order to make best use of the morning light for a few photos. I had even brought along my brand new camera for its first trip out. It wasn't really a Christmas present though it had arrived just before Christmas, and I was quite excited until I remembered that the last time I had a new camera we also had a walk out on Rough Tor, and the camera stopped working before I got to the top of the hill!

Well, today we were in luck. My camera worked for the entire day without any glitches, and Sarah made it to the top of Brown Willy. Both Rough Tor and Brown Willy are superb hills with fantastic views; what is particularly appealing about them both is their wonderfully shaped craggy summits. Brown Willy is particularly distinctive, with its ridge of

We didn't see much wildlife, but the ponies provided some animal interest.

knobbly peaks visible from as far away as the A30. Both hills have granite tors at their peaks, and a scattering of rocks around them. The formation of these shaped peaks commenced in the Ice Ages, when the granite and surrounding landscape were repeatedly frozen and thawed. Rocks would shatter and slip down from the summit in regular landslips, leaving them scattered around on the slopes. Bare ground would be stripped from the summits, leaving just the most solid hard rock behind; these would gradually be weathered by wind and rain into the sculptures we see today.

By lunchtime we were back in the car-park, which had been transformed from a deserted spot into a busy thoroughfare. Boxing Day seems to be the day that everyone heads out into the countryside to walk off the excesses of the day before. I am always more amused by watching people than wildlife on Boxing Day, which is a good job really since all I saw on the moor were ravens, buzzards and a meadow pipit.

In the car-park, which was now full, I saw lots of Christmas presents going out for their first-ever walk. There were a couple of kites, a few new coats, and lots of matching scarf, hat and glove sets! Never again, for another year, will we see this many matching accoutrements. Experience tells me that there is some sort of a law, which states that we can go through many years of life without losing gloves, but as soon as we get a matching set of accessories we will, within days, lose a glove on a walk, in a drawer or in the pocket of a little-used coat. I wonder how many of those sets made it back to their cars today?

Our view looking back to Rough Tor as we ascended Brown Willy (left).

Sarah holds on to the triangulation point at the top of Brown Willy, and achieves a life-long goal (above).

Part of the granite ridge – such a distinctive feature of Brown Willy – with Rough Tor in the distance (below).

The next part of our day was going to include a trip to Davidstow airfield. This is an excellent place to see wading birds, particularly during the late summer and early autumn, but today I was hoping to see golden plover there. No sooner had we left the car-park at Rough Tor than we realized that not all of these people were here just for the fresh air and a walk. Along the road between Rough Tor and Davidstow we must have passed at least twenty horse boxes and 100 four-wheel drive vehicles. It was, of course, the Boxing Day hunt. On Davidstow, we caught sight of the hunt disappearing over the horizon followed by a range of four-wheel drives and

The summit of Rough Tor, with its huge granite tors (above). When we returned, the car-park was full (below), and a queue of people were tackling Rough Tor.

quads; not much chance that there would be any birds in the area now!

Our final plan for the day was to wait until late afternoon to watch the starlings coming in to roost. This area plays host to the largest such roost in Cornwall, and during the winter as many as a million birds might come here to find sanctuary in the pine trees between Crowdy and Davidstow. We took up posi-

tion near Davidstow airfield and adjacent to the pines, where I watched the birds roosting last year. We waited and we waited. The time was about 4.30 p.m. when I looked to the south-east and saw masses of starlings flying in their characteristically varied drawn-out shapes. But they weren't coming to the woods near us, they were heading for somewhere over

A flock of starlings flies to the roost near Crowdy Reservoir (above).
Davidstow airfield (below left) is a good place to see wading birds,
particularly in early autumn. I took this photo of a juvenile ruff (below right)
on my last trip to Davidstow airfield, in September.

towards Rough Tor. We drove back
along the road to the car-park at Crowdy
Reservoir to see the last few small flocks
disappearing out of sight into some distant pines.

December 31st

The Tail is Red

It is with some trepidation that I make this the final chapter in *A Cornish Year*, because I wouldn't like you to remember me for all the wrong reasons. So before you start reading this section, I want you to know that I have never before – and will probably never again – agreed to go and see a bird round the back of the public toilets. But I must confess that this is exactly what I did today.

The small, fifteenth-century church in Gunwalloe, dedicated to St Winwaloe.

You will remember my friend Steve Jones, because he took me to see the damselflies at Great Wheal Seton in June. (He was the one with the latex gloves.) Well, he phoned me last night and told me about a black redstart that was frequenting the toilet block at Gunwalloe on the Lizard. Like me, he is not one to feel self-conscious when it comes to nature watching, and when he found a black redstart that was happy to come within about a metre of him, he obviously got out his camera and started photographing it, regardless of the possible comments from passers-by.

Happily, as well as being a knowledgeable naturalist and a good photographer, Steve is also generous with his findings, so he called to let me know about this obliging bird. He knew I wouldn't be able to resist a close encounter of the bird kind, so there was just a small doubt in the back of my mind that it could be a set-up. I wondered whether I might get to the toilet block, mount my big lens on a tripod outside the gents' entrance, and meet some burley bloke who would punch me first and ask questions later. Or maybe Steve would be hiding in the undergrowth to take photos of me taking photos outside the gents' loo.

Fortunately, there wasn't a big burley bloke, and I didn't make the *News of the World* the next day. Unfortunately, there wasn't a black redstart either, so my relief was tempered by disappointment, and I took the dog for a run on the beach instead. Remembering the uncanny white-breasted robin tip-off from the Revd Andrew Hill, I decided it might be

A rather beautiful female black redstart (top). The black redstart, as well as having a reddish-coloured rump, has whitish fringing to some of its wing feathers, which can be seen in the photograph above.

The attractive cove of Gunwalloe (above).
A female stonechat that was associating with the black redstart (below).

worth visiting the wonderful little church on the beach to ask for guidance from on high. Sure enough, on the way back past the gents' toilets, I decided to take a look in the field opposite; lo and behold there she was, the bird of my prayers: a wonderful, female black redstart. I knew it was the same bird that Steve had told me about because she hopped right up to me when I got out my camera.

Black redstarts are not a proper Cornish bird, in that they don't breed in the county. However, they probably occur more frequently in Cornwall than in any other county in Britain, because they migrate westwards from their breeding grounds to seek a milder climate for autumn and winter. They are also quite unusual birds in the places they tend to hang out, as you might already have gathered! In the south-east of Britain, for example, they breed on waste ground, ruined buildings, and around power stations. Strangely enough, like the avocet seen in February, this is another bird which benefited from the Second World War, when many built-up areas in the south-east of England were turned into bomb sites.

In late October, we see a major influx of black redstarts from eastern Europe, and many stay over winter. They like beaches, particularly strandlines with plenty of insects, and built-up areas near the coast. They can be seen just about anywhere in the county, but are not well known by many people, so this is the one bird I am asked to identify most frequently by people in November, who have seen something unusual in their gardens.

Epilogue

A typical day in July: rain and a howling gale, but I'm not complaining, the light was fantastic!!

It's New Year's Eve, and instead of heading out to celebrate the New Year I am reflecting on a wonderful year.

I feel incredibly privileged to have been able to take part in such a wide range of activities, and meet such a lot of knowledgeable, dedicated and friendly people. It's difficult to pick out the highlights of the year, but for moments of sheer joy I am taken back to the grey seal release; listening to greater horseshoe bats, and photographing dormice. In terms of admiration, I have to hand it to the volunteers who record and monitor the dolphins found washed up on our shore; the people who collect seal pups from all parts of the county; those who work physically hard to protect our wildlife habitats, and those who lead guided walks and head specialist groups, happy to share their knowledge with anyone who shows an interest.

The one thing that has struck me more than any other is the sheer number of people and organizations in the county working for wildlife. Whether your interest is in flowers, rocks, birds, conservation work or any other aspect of our natural history, there is something for you to get involved with. One of the best ways to learn about the different groups is to become a member of CWT, but

We can take part in a vast range of activities, like rock-pooling at Durgan.

I have put together a rather large appendix to give more information about those aspects covered in *A Cornish Year*.

Apart from the changing seasons, the factor that seems to have had the greatest influence on my activities is the weather. In this regard, I think I must have chosen one of the worst years ever! The summer was extraordinarily wet and windy: look no further than the photos accompanying the Pentire and The Rumps walk to demonstrate the changeable conditions that prevailed in July; what a day that was! The most obvious impact of this was on butterflies, with a real paucity of several species made worse by the fact that last summer was also a bad one; let's hope next year is better.

When I wanted wet weather for a fungus foray, it was dry for a week; when I wanted calm and cloudy for a moth-watching evening, it was clear and moonlit; when I wanted dry weather for a dawn chorus, I got a downpour, and when I wanted a wind for sailing, I was becalmed! But really, I wouldn't want it any other way. The changing seasons and changeable weather both help to make Cornwall such a special place. It might often be dull and cloudy, but it isn't often dull and boring!

Tonight I should be adding up my yearly bird list, but I must confess that I didn't keep one. Year lists and life lists don't excite me like they once did; there are far more important things to do. But that won't stop me getting out early tomorrow morning, come rain or shine, to see as many birds as I can on New Year's Day – some habits die hard!

Appendix

Here is further information on the locations, sightings and contact details for organizations mentioned in the book. The most frequently mentioned wildlife organizations are listed on page 192.

Jan 1: A Twitch in Time

My list of birds seen on New Year's Day 2008 (in order of recording): house sparrow; blackbird; dunnock; blue tit; carrion crow; robin; chaffinch; pheasant; greenfinch; goldfinch; jackdaw; great tit; bullfinch; collared dove; buzzard; wren; rook; song thrush; wood pigeon; herring gull; meadow pipit; long-tailed tit; great spotted woodpecker; goldcrest; raven; chiffchaff; jay; starling; redwing; moorhen; magpie; grey wagtail; cormorant; mistle thrush; black-headed gull; pied wagtail; lapwing; grey heron; wigeon; teal; redshank; curlew; great black-backed gull; lesser black-backed gull; dunlin; golden plover; shelduck; Mediterranean gull; oystercatcher; green-winged teal; little egret; linnet; mute swan; ringed plover; grey plover; sanderling; turnstone; great northern diver; little grebe; shag; rock pipit; bar-tailed godwit; skylark. My walk was from Relubbus (SW 567 319) to Carnsew Pool (SW 555 374), along the River Hayle.

Jan 3: Cattle Egrets

The cattle egrets stayed in Cornwall a few weeks, diminishing in numbers through the spring. They didn't breed here, but a pair bred in Somerset – the first recorded in Britain. (The following winter saw another influx, though fewer in number.)

For updates on bird sightings, see the specialist websites on page 192.

Jan 17: A Tip from the Top

I had quite an interesting year for birds with plumage abnormalities: a pure white linnet on Nare Point (Helford); a peculiar black-and-white blackbird on The Garrison, St Mary's; lots of almost black pheasants; a leucistic moorhen at Slimbridge (I do leave Cornwall!).

Jan 26: The Big Garden Birdwatch

For more on the Big Garden Birdwatch, see www.rspb.org.uk/birdwatch.

The survey results from Jenny's garden in St Just were: house sparrow: 15; starling: 10; chaffinch: 7; jackdaw: 4; great tit: 2; magpie: 1; goldfinch: 1; robin: 1; rook: 1.

Results from the RSPB showed 5,000 people in Cornwall took part in the Big Garden Birdwatch. The top 10 Cornish birds were: chaffinch; house sparrow, starling; blue tit; blackbird; greenfinch; robin; great tit; goldfinch; jackdaw. The house sparrow was knocked off top spot, reflecting its continued decline, down by two-thirds in 30 years.

Feb 2: Raindrops on Snowdrops

For more about Pencarrow House, opening times and events, see www.pencarrow.co.uk, or tel 01208 841369.

Feb 5: Just Cruising

For more about Tamar birdwatching cruises, see www.tamarcruising.com, or tel Tamar Cruising: 01752 822105.

Feb 7: A Seal's Approval

The grey seals released were: Malcomina ('Mina'), yellow tag on back right flipper, no. 02, female; Twister, orange tag on back right flipper, no. 66801, female; Hocken, yellow tag on back left flipper, no. 06, male; Kitto, yellow tag on back left flipper, no. 03, male. (Males are always tagged on the back left, females on the back right flippers.)

Mina and Kitto were later recorded by the Cornwall Seal Group at Mutton Cove until 24 Feb. Then they disappeared from the area, which is usual for post-weaning seals, since many explore the area around them to learn where they live. So Cornish seals can be found as far away as SW Ireland, Wales, or France; we have evidence from records of tagged animals.

If you find a white-coated seal pup on the beach, alone and in distress:

1 *Keep your distance:* a white-coated pup feeds from its mother; she won't return if people are close.
2 *Do not handle it:* for your safety and the seal's.
3 If it is thin, injured or seems unwell (noisy breathing, coughing, runny nose), it probably needs help. Tel the National Seal Sanctuary: 01326 221361, or an RSPCA officer.

Mutton Cove is at SW 583 433.

For more about seals and the work of the National Seal Sanctuary, see www.sealsanctuary.co.uk. For more about seals in Cornwall, or to get involved in their protection, see Cornwall Seal Group: www.cornwallsealgroup.co.uk.

Feb 14: Love is in the Air

The Lost Gardens of Heligan are open daily except Christmas Eve and Christmas Day, 10 a.m. to 5 p.m. (Nov–Feb), and 10 a.m. to 6 p.m. (March–Oct). See www.heligan.com; tel 01726 845101.

Feb 15: From Croaks to Crocuses

Living Churchyards Project and churchyard events, see CWT website. Churchyards good for natural history include:

- *Devoran:* Good for wildflowers.
- *Gunwalloe:* Fantastic dunes setting, typical coastal wildflowers.
- *Herodsfoot:* Wildflowers attract the marbled white butterfly, quite rare in Cornwall.
- *Kenwyn:* Varied trees and birds.
- *Lanteglos-by-Fowey:* Wild daffodils.
- *Lelant:* Excellent wildflower meadow, orchids, many insects, including Red Data Book species of miner bee (*Andrina hattorfiana*).
- *Minster:* SSI, due to greater horseshoe bat roost.
- *Old Kea:* Snowdrops Jan/Feb; the most remarkable place.
- *Philleigh:* Good for roosting bats.
- *Temple:* Good for wild daffodils in spring, summer wildflowers.
- *Tintagel:* Great for lichens, thrift, unimproved grassland.

Feb 26: Scandal of the Killing Nets

If you find a dead cetacean, or turtle, in Cornwall, tel the Wildlife Trust's strandings hotline: 0845 2012626. If you find a live stranding, tel British Divers Marine Life Rescue: 01825 765546. For more on strandings volunteers: www.cornwallwildlifetruststrandings.org.

Other things to do: avoid eating bass, unless hand-line caught; in the SW such fish are identified by tagging. When buying fish, ask where and how it was caught. Write to your MP and MEPs to ask for bass to become a quota fish, and for a European ban on pair-trawling for bass. Buy only fish from sustainable stocks; for a list, see the Marine Conservation Society's website: www.fishonline.org.

March 19: From the Caribbean...

James and Dink survived. They were flown to Gran Canaria on 23 June, and released into the wild two days later.

The Blue Reef Aquarium is in Newquay: www.bluereefaquarium.co.uk; tel 01637 878134.

March 24: The Great Easter Egg Hunt

Rory Goodall leads land-based and marine trips (on a RIB), and organizes holidays. See his website: www.elementaltours.co.uk.

For more on the identification of the egg-cases of sharks, skates and rays, as well as the work of the Shark Trust, see www.sharktrust.org.

April 4: A Date with a High Society

Dobwalls Bypass Statistics: 1½ ml long; cost £42m; work on the road began winter 2006; opened fully later than planned, Dec 2008. It is hoped that the 21,000 vehicles previously travelling through Dobwalls will be reduced by 90 per cent. Wildlife mitigation includes an otter ledge; two dedicated bat bridges; a badger tunnel, and a fish pass. £325,000 was spent on the bat bridges; approximately 50,000 native trees were planted along its verges; 1½ ml of Cornish hedges were constructed.

April 21: Soft Furnishings

For details to make nest boxes for garden birds, see www.lincstrust.org.uk/factsheets/nestbox.php.

May 14: A Scilly Holiday

Visit the Scillies by air or sea. Flights are by helicopter from Penzance, or by plane from Land's End (or Newquay, Exeter, Bristol and Southampton in summer). The ferry from Penzance takes longer but, for good sailors, is the most interesting means of travel, with views of birds and cetaceans while at sea. For details of ferries and planes, tel 0845 7105555, or see www.ios-travel.co.uk; for the helicopter, tel 01736 363871. Boat trips to off-islands are regular, except in winter; there is a good bus service around St Mary's. For accommodation, tel tourist information on St Mary's: 01720 422536, or see www.simplyscilly.co.uk.

To visit the islands to undertake voluntary conservation work, or to support the Isles of Scilly Wildlife Trust by becoming a member or making a donation, contact them at Carn Thomas, St Mary's, Isles of Scilly, TR21 0PT; tel 01720 422153, or see www.ios-wildlifetrust.org.uk.

May 25: Up at Dawn...

Immediately after this dawn chorus walk, I bought a digital voice recorder. It has transformed my wildlife experience: I carry it wherever I go, and copy the sounds on to my laptop, to share with audiences at talks.

The maximum weight of a dormouse on the day of this survey was 21 g, in contrast to the maximum weight of 36 g for one found in autumn. This gives an idea of the weight lost by a dormouse in hibernation. To find out about guided walks to see dormice, join the CWT and see the diary of dates in their magazine, *Wild Cornwall*. Similar events may be organized by CC, details of which can usually be found in their annually produced *Countryside Events Diary*.

June 3: Clovers at the Drop of a Hat

Land around Caerthillian Cove is managed by Natural England. Grazing animals encourage clovers, many other flowers, and birds, including choughs. Reach it on foot from the National Trust car-park at Kynance Cove, or from Lizard village. The best place for clovers is the south-facing slope of the spur of land between the two small valleys leading to the cove: SW 696 125.

The 10 clovers we saw on here are: western clover, *Trifolium occidentale**; rough clover, *Trifolium scabrum*; lesser trefoil, *Trifolium dubium**; upright clover, *Trifolium strictum*; slender trefoil, *Trifolium micranthum**; twin-flowered clover, *Trifolium bocconei*; knotted clover, *Trifolium striatum**; white clover, *Trifolium repens*; hop trefoil, *Trifolium campestre*; burrowing clover, *Trifolium subterraneum**. Species marked * are those I could cover with a hat at one time.

If you would like to record wildflowers in your area, or visit interesting locations with knowledgeable experts, contact the Botanical Cornwall Group: www.floracam.co.uk/bcg.

June 7: A Moonlit Flit

From 9.30 p.m. to 11.30 p.m., we saw 19 species of moth, roughly in the following order: silver-ground carpet; green carpet; common marbled carpet; small angle shades; scalloped hazel; flame shoulder; brimstone; brown silver-line; common wave; rivulet; pale tussock; broken-barred carpet; plain golden-Y; peach blossom; heart and dart; yellow-barred brindle; peppered; broom and coxcomb prominent. For more about National Moth Night, including events in your area, see www.nationalmothnight.info.

For details about Atropos, see www.atropos.info. For more about Butterfly Conservation, see www.butterfly-conservsation.org.

June 10: Bats in the Belfry

For more about bats and work done to protect them, see the Bat Conservation

Trust: www.bats.org.uk, or Cornwall Bat Group: www.cornwall-batgroup.co.uk.

June 11: The Rule of Bird Surveying
The Breeding Bird Survey has been used to establish lists of breeding birds threatened in the UK. There are 3 categories: the 'Red' list for species which have declined by 50 per cent or more in the last 25 years (or are threatened for some other specific reason); the 'Amber' list for species which have declined by 25–49 per cent in the last 25 years (with other possible criteria for inclusion), and the 'Green' list for the rest.

Some surprising birds that are Red-listed include: skylark, song thrush, spotted flycatcher, marsh tit, house sparrow, starling, linnet, bullfinch, yellowhammer and reed bunting.

For more on the British Trust for Ornithology, the other surveys and the work they do, see www.bto.org.

June 17: A Sea Safari
These trips operate throughout the year, leaving from the quay beside the National Maritime Museum Cornwall, in Falmouth. Prices might seem a little expensive, but each ticket includes a free entry into the Museum on the same day, and trips operate even if only a few people book them; there were only five people on the trip I took. Each person is provided with a warm, waterproof outer layer of clothing, a life-jacket and binoculars. To keep up to date with sightings, there is a page on their website, and you can receive emails informing of special creatures seen from the boat. For details of prices and booking, see: www.kingharryscornwall.co.uk/ferries/orca, or tel 01872 861910.

June 19: Choughed to Bits
The choughs breed near Lizard Point. From the car-park near the lighthouse, or at the most southerly point, walk west along the Coast Path for about 90 metres. Usually a group of people is watching them, so they shouldn't be difficult to find in June. The best time

is when the young have just fledged – from the start of June to the second or third week of the month. In the third week, you should see young birds and adults together.

June 22: Damsels and Dragons
The 11 species we recorded were: *Damselflies:* scarce blue-tailed; small red; blue-tailed; azure; large red; beautiful demoiselle. *'True' dragonflies:* emperor; keeled skimmer; broad-bodied chaser; common darter; four-spotted chaser.

The complete list of dragonflies found breeding in Cornwall, organized according to rarity, is as follows.
- *Common:* beautiful demoiselle; large red damselfly; blue-tailed damselfly; common blue damselfly; azure damselfly; southern hawker; golden-ringed dragonfly; common darter; emperor dragonfly; broad-bodied chaser; four-spotted chaser.
- *Locally common:* emerald damselfly; common hawker; migrant hawker; black-tailed skimmer; keeled skimmer; black darter.
- *Scarce, rare, or found in only a small number of localities:* banded demoiselle; white-legged damselfly; scarce blue-tailed damselfly; small red damselfly; lesser emperor; red-veined darter; ruddy darter.

To become more involved in recording dragonflies, contact the British Dragonfly Society, see: www.dragonflysoc.org.uk. This gives information about current projects; the latest dragonfly news; details about recording, and details for county recorders.

July 1: A DIY Guided Walk
This walk is 6 ml long, and takes about 3 hours. It begins at West Pentire (SW 776 607), follows the Coast Path via Porth Joke (SW 773 604) to Holywell (SW 767 590), and then cuts inland beside the golf course across The Kelseys, returning to West Pentire. For details of this and other National Trust guided walks, see www.nationaltrust.org.uk.

I saw 10 species of butterfly: dark green fritillary; silver-studded blue; small heath; small white; ringlet; meadow brown; small skipper; red admiral; painted lady and gatekeeper, and plenty of six-spot burnet moths.

July 2: Huffin and Puffin...

The walks around Pentire and The Rumps are organized by a group of friends who used to do the walk themselves, and thought it would be nice to lead others. The walks are free, with donations accepted for a charity or local wildlife project. They are every Wednesday, May–July, 10 a.m. to 3 p.m., from Pentire Farm (SW 936 803), near Polzeath. Check that they are operating: there is a regular advert in the North Cornwall Advertiser, or tel the Tourist Information Centre, Bodmin: 01208 76616.

July 7: Ratty Comes Home

If the reintroduction receives public support, and funding is found to continue this project, water voles may be reintroduced to the River Hayle area. Details should be available in the local press, or from the CWT website.

If a reintroduction has taken place, here are tips for identifying the presence of water voles along a river: look for the holes they make in river banks, and for the chewed remains of vegetation close to the water – short stumps of grass often cut off diagonally, or the tougher parts of plants they have discarded; water voles often leave their droppings in piles, or latrines – the droppings are cylindrical with blunt ends; listen for the distinctive 'plopping' sound as a water vole enters the water.

July 13: Spraint Sniffing

Information about CWT local groups and their activities is in the CWT magazine, Wild Cornwall, sent to all members. Within the magazine is a diary listing hundreds of walks and events each year. See the CWT website for membership details.

July 18: A Life on the Ocean Wave

The RSPB has a member of staff on the Scillonian each Friday through the summer season to help travellers look for seabirds and cetaceans. On these days, members of the RSPB get reduced-price fares. There are occasional days with the same arrangement for CWT members. To book a trip on the Scillonian, tel 0845 7105555; for more information, see www.ios-travel.co.uk.

July 22: ... the Queen's Jubilee

The Jubilee Queen does trips to sea from Padstow around Pentire Point, The Rumps and the two offshore islands each day, normally several times a day, in summer. Times are detailed daily on noticeboards around Padstow harbour. The boat sails from a couple of places close to the harbour, which are well signed. If you are going to Padstow especially for a trip, tel in advance: 01841 521093, though exact times are not usually determined until the morning, when the weather can be assessed. There are also trips up the River Camel to Wadebridge on high spring tides.

Aug 20: The Helford

The Helford Voluntary Marine Conservation Group organizes many events in the area through the year, including an annual boat trip on the river. Membership of the group is inexpensive. For details, or to take part in its activities, see its website.

Trebah Garden, nr Mawnan Smith, is privately owned. It is open daily, 10.30 a.m. to 5 p.m. See www.trebah-garden.co.uk, or tel 01326 250448.

Glendurgan Garden, nr Mawnan Smith, is owned by the National Trust, and is open Feb–Oct, Tues–Sat, 10.30 a.m. to 5.30 p.m. See www.nationaltrust.org.uk/devoncornwall, or tel 01872 862090.

Aug 22: Basking in the Sun

The 2008 basking shark survey ran from 15 June to 24 Aug. For 4 weeks it was at Gwennap Head, then at Carn

Gloose from 15 July. For more about the SeaWatch project, see www.sea-watch-sw.org.

To get involved in surveys for basking sharks, see the CWT website.

Aug 23: Hide-and-Seek

CWT has specialist groups, including the photographic group, which meets monthly indoors for talks, critiques and reviews. It organizes regular field trips to photograph a variety of wildlife in Cornwall. See the CWT website.

Walmsley Sanctuary is a Cornwall Birds reserve; access is for members only. It is on the Wadebridge–Rock road at SW 990 745. Park just before Trewornan Bridge, a narrow bridge with traffic lights, and take the footpath to the right just after the bridge. Membership of the society is inexpensive and worthwhile for keen birdwatchers.

Sept 6: The Reptile Challenge

Access to the dunes between Perranporth and Holywell is at the south end and along the Coast Path. The area described, at the north end, is owned by the Ministry of Defence; casual access is not permitted. For visits to this area, look out for guided walks, publicized in CWT's magazine *Wild Cornwall* and CC's *Countryside Events Diary*. Reptile and amphibian walks are organized by Cornwall's Reptile and Amphibian Group (CRAG), and publicized in *Wild Cornwall*.

Oct 5: Hawking

Experiences with birds of prey are available through established centres, such as the Screech Owl Sanctuary on Goss Moor. See www.screechowlsanctuary.co.uk.

Oct 11: Up the Creek without a Paddle

Among the ways to explore Carrick Roads, is a good ferry service between Falmouth and Truro, which stops at Trelissick and Smuggler's Cottage. See www.falriverlinks.co.uk.

Oct 13: A Walk in the Woods

For more about the work of the Woodland Trust, see their website. For details of the Friends of Kilminorth, see www.friendsofkilminorthwoods.co.uk. To visit Trenant Wood, there is a small car-park near Polpever. From Duloe, head south; take the minor road right to Tredinnick. Continue to a five-way road junction. Here, take the extremely narrow road to Polpever (look for the Woodland Trust sign). Continue along this track, past the right turning into the hamlet of Polpever, along an unmade stretch of track into the Woodland Trust car-park at SX 237 551. From here, take an access path to the Woodland Trust land. On the land, there are several paths and tracks to follow. You shouldn't get lost if you remember the topography of the land, though it is a large area! There are no facilities, so come prepared.

Oct 15: Smoke Gets in my Eyes

To take part in conservation work anywhere in the county, tel BTCV: 01209 610610; or see www.btcv.org.

Steeple Woods LNR is owned by CC. The Steeple Woodland Project Group meets every Sunday at 2 p.m. at the main gate into the reserve from Steeple Lane to undertake practical conservation work; all welcome.

Oct 25: Fungus Foray

For more about the Cornwall Fungus Recording Group, email Pauline Penna on ppenna@dsl.pipex.com.

For a full list of events led by CC and other organizations, see the *Countryside Events Diary*, or their website.

Dec 14: Cake at Coverack

For more about the geology of Cornwall, see the website of the Cornwall Regionally Important Geological/Geomorphological Sites (RIGS) group: www.cornwallrigs.org.uk.

Dec 23: Snowy for Christmas

I believe this snowy owl was the third record for Cornwall, the first since 1945.

No wonder it attracted such interest. For updates on the latest birds seen in Cornwall, use one of the websites listed below.

Dec 26: Pinnacle of a Cornish Year
Approach Brown Willy from the car-park for Rough Tor, SX 138 819. The starling roost can be in the pines between Crowdy and Davidstow, or along the northern fringe of Roughtor Moor. Probably the best place to watch is from the car-park at Crowdy Reservoir, SX 139 833.

Dec 31: The Tail is Red
Gunwalloe Church Cove is at SW 661 205, accessed at the end of a minor road off the A3083 (Helston–Lizard) nr RNAS Culdrose.

Organizations and Publications
The following organizations manage nature reserves, and lead countryside events in Cornwall:

- **Cornwall Council** (CC), Environment & Heritage section, Cornwall Council, Old County Hall, Truro; tel 01872 222000; www.cornwall.gov. uk. Produces annual *Countryside Events Diary*, available from tourist information centres, etc.
- **Cornwall Birds** (Cornwall Bird-Watching & Preservation Society): www.cbwps.org.uk. Has own magazine, detailing guided walks, and annual bird report for members.
- **Cornwall Wildlife Trust** (CWT), Five Acres, Allet, nr Truro TR4 9DJ; tel: 01872 273939, www.cornwall-wildlifetrust.org.uk. Magazine, *Wild Cornwall*, details events organized by its specialist and local groups.
- **Helford Voluntary Marine Conservation Area** (HVMCA) is managed to protect the marine environment around the Helford Estuary. It organizes events through the year. See www.helfordmarineconservation.co.uk. Details of walks are also in a leaflet distributed to members and through local outlets.

- **Isles of Scilly Wildlife Trust**, Carn Thomas, St Mary's, Isles of Scilly TR21 0PT; tel: 01720 422153; www.ios-wildlifetrust.org.uk. Shares magazine and events diary with CWT.
- **National Trust**, Cornwall Office, Lanhydrock, Bodmin PL30 4DE; tel: 01208 74281; www.national-trust.org.uk. Events organized from different properties.
- **Natural England**, Cornwall and Isles of Scilly Team, Trevint House, Strangways Villas, Truro, Cornwall TR1 2PA; tel: 01872 265710; head office 01733 455000; www.naturalengland.org.uk.
- **Royal Society for the Protection of Birds** (RSPB), South West Regional Office, Keble House, Southernhay Gardens, Exeter, Devon EX1 1NT; tel: 01392 432691; www.rspb.org. uk. Local group in Cornwall.
- **The Woodland Trust**: www.woodland-trust.org.uk.

Wildlife Information Websites
There is an independent wildlife e-news service. Unsolicited emails pass between members with news of wildlife sightings, questions and answers. See http://groups.yahoo.com/group/CornishWildlife/.

For daily news of birds spotted in Cornwall, visit: www.cornwall-birding.co.uk, or www.sennen-cove.com.

For national news of bird sightings, updated frequently during the day, try: www.birdguides.com.

About David Chapman
David's website, showcasing his photographs, books, writing and much more, is at: www.davidchapman.org. uk. David gives talks to groups, including on the theme of 'A Cornish Year', featuring many photographs and some sound recordings, including the incredible greater horseshoe bats. To book a talk, contact David via his website, or tel 01736 850287.